Jacob Biggle

Biggle Cow Book

Jacob Biggle

Biggle Cow Book

ISBN/EAN: 9783337182267

Printed in Europe, USA, Canada, Australia, Japan

Cover: Foto ©Andreas Hilbeck / pixelio.de

More available books at **www.hansebooks.com**

AYRSHIRES IN SCOTLAND.

BIGGLE COW BOOK

OLD TIME AND MODERN COW-LORE

RECTIFIED, CONCENTRATED AND RECORDED

FOR THE BENEFIT OF MAN

BY

JACOB BIGGLE

———

ILLUSTRATED

———

"The man who does not love a cow
Is but a poor stick anyhow."

———

PHILADELPHIA
WILMER ATKINSON CO.
1898

CONTENTS.

		PAGE
List of Colored Plates		6
Preface		7
Chart Showing External Cow		9
Chapter I.	Statistics	11
Chapter II.	Breeds	13
Chapter III.	The Bull	21
Chapter IV.	Mother Cow	23
Chapter V.	Baby	31
Chapter VI.	The Heifer	35
Chapter VII.	The Ox	37
Chapter VIII.	Food and Drink	39
Chapter IX.	Food and Drink, (*Continued*)	47
Chapter X.	The Barn	53
Chapter XI.	Stable Requisites	59
Chapter XII.	The Good Milker	63
Chapter XIII.	Milk and Cream	67
Chapter XIV	Butter	73
Chapter XV.	Imitations	81
Chapter XVI.	Cheese	83
Chapter XVII.	Beef	89
Chapter XVIII.	By-Products	93
Chapter XIX.	Winter	99
Chapter XX.	Points on Markets	103
Chapter XXI.	Dairy Appliances	109
Chapter XXII.	Public Creamery	117
Chapter XXIII.	Villager's One Cow	123
Chapter XXIV.	The Milk Farm	127
Chapter XXV	Ailments and Remedies	131
Chapter XXVI.	Round-up	141
Index		144

LIST OF COLORED PLATES.

PLATE I.   JERSEY COW.

PLATE II.   GUERNSEY COW.

PLATE III.   AYRSHIRE COW.

PLATE IV.   HOLSTEIN-FRIESIAN COW.

PLATE V.   HEREFORD COW.

PLATE VI.   SHORTHORN COW.

PLATE VII.   GALLOWAY COW.

PLATE VIII. RED POLLED COW.

"The lowing herd winds slowly o'er the lea."

PREFACE.

The dairy business is undergoing rapid changes the world over; nowhere more rapidly than in America. The invention and perfection of the separator have hastened the establishment of the factory system, and the creamery is in successful operation everywhere. Feeding has been reduced to a simple and exact science as a result of the joint work of agricultural chemists and practical dairymen. The silo is appearing on farm after farm. The silage crops will presently increase in number, and will include peas and beans as well as corn and other grasses.

The bacteria of ferments have been subjected to commercial harness, and put to work. Butter flavor is under control.

Reliable milk testing apparatus is on the market, and fat percentages can be ascertained quickly and cheaply.

The science of cattle breeding is receiving more and more attention, and we now have a considerable number of herd books on this side of the Atlantic.

There will be a steady improvement in American dairy stock from this time forward.

No ambitious young American need be ashamed to choose dairying for a profession, for it is as much of a profession in fact as any calling now practised in this country. It takes good brains, good judgment and long experience to make the most of it. Dairying has a great future, I am sure, and it need not be cast aside even by young men who have promised themselves future fame and riches. It is a noble calling.

There has been a great awakening to the fact that the dairy cow is a most reliable source of farm profits. Dairy profits are in one sense small, but they are unremitting. There is never an interruption in the demand for wholesome human food. Total dairy products of the United States far outrival the gold output of all the mines of the world.

The publishers ask me to extend their thanks to D. H. Goodell, O. D. Munn, S. Mather & Sons, W. M. Beninger, Ezra Michener, K. B. Armour, Smiths & Powell Co., J. D. Avery, S. M. Winslow, J. Cheston Morris, M. D., S. P. Clarke, Moseley & Stoddard Mfg. Co., and other kind friends who have furnished them with photographs of the breeds in which they are interested. Nearly all the illustrations of animals are reproductions of photographs. The colored plates were painted by a skilled live stock artist, and faithfully show the leading breeds they represent.

May every cow owner find this little book to be a guide and helper in the coming years.   J. B.

Reference Chart
Showing Parts of the External Cow.

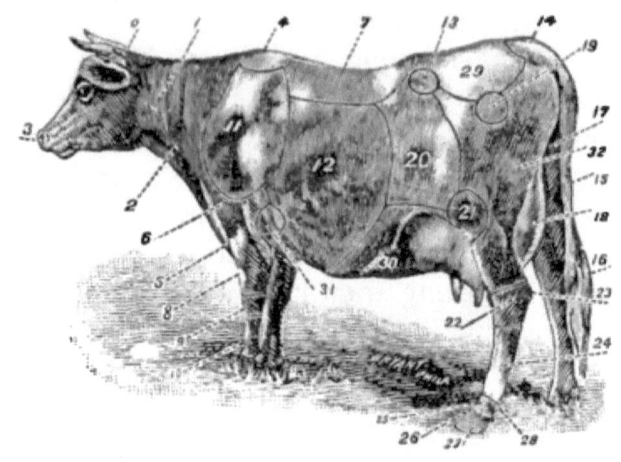

0	Poll	17	Escutcheon
1	Neck	18	Udder
2	Jugular Gutter	19	Hip Joint
3	Muzzle	20	Flank
4	Withers	21	Stifle-joint
5	Dewlap	22	Hock
6	Point of Shoulder	23	Point of Hock
7	Back	24	Cannon
8	Forearm	25	Foot
9	Knee	26	Coronet
10	Cannon	27	Claw
11	Shoulder	28	Ergot
12	Side of Chest	29	Croup
13	Angle of Haunch	30	Belly
14	Root of Tail	31	Elbow
15	Tail	32	Buttock.
16	Switch		

Photograph by Davison, Kansas City.

THE NOON HOUR.

Chapter I.

STATISTICS.

"The cattle upon a thousand hills."

Great is the dairy cow! Hail to her! But if she give less than 5000 pounds of milk per year, or 200 pounds of butter, away with her! She is not profitable.

And yet the average cow of the United States gives less than 2800 pounds of milk per year.

There are fifteen to twenty millions of dairy cows in the United States; and enough other cattle to make a grand total of over fifty million head. This, of course, includes bulls, oxen, young stock, and the great herds of steers which roam the plains of the West.

There are about half a million thoroughbreds in the country, eight million (half or higher) grades, and more than forty million "scrubs," so called.. (I prefer to speak of them as natives; and yet some of them are "scrubs" in fact.)

There are about fifteen million calves born every year in the United States.

The average value of the dairy cow, take the country over, is only about $22.50. Curiously enough, the smallest state in the Union has the highest priced cows—$38.33, average. This tells of good dairying in Rhode Island.

As to the total dairy and beef products of the United States, per annum, the figures are so large as to be bewildering. The gold-hunters find only two hundred million a year, while a single by-product of American cattle (the manure) is rated as worth more than that amount of money! It is surer than gold, too.

The cows of the United States yield five thousand million gallons of milk per year, the butter product is a billion pounds, and the product of cheese two hundred and fifty million pounds—grand figures, indeed, and enough to make us vain.

But to be officially informed that we send abroad more oleomargarine than butter does not lead to vanity but toward mortification. The 4,500,000 farms of the United States should be flavoring Europe's bread with good butter and cheese.

There are now about 5000 creameries and cheese factories in the United States. They have sprung up, for the most part, within a quarter of a century, and their number is rapidly increasing. Dairying, as a business, is making rapid strides in this country.

Chapter II.

BREEDS.

The thoroughbred animal is a good home missionary; it teaches a better way.—Tim.

The more important of the thoroughbred cattle in the United States are here briefly described.

Full descriptions of the points which are considered essential in judging the different breeds are usually to be found in the herd books issued by the respective breeders' associations. A list of the present secretaries of the leading clubs and associations will be found at the end of the book.

JERSEY. Origin, Channel Islands. Average weight of cow, 800 pounds. Purpose, butter. Color, "gray-fawn and white, yellow-fawn and white, gray-dun and white, gray and white, silver-gray dun, cream-color, fawn," etc. Often dark-colored on nose and legs. The Jersey is characterized by "neatness of form, slender frame, deer-like head, and gentleness." No cow is higher in American favor. See colored Plate I.

"*Of all the creatures the farm can boast,—*
And in my time I've seen a host,—
The dearest one to me I trow,
And pet of the place, is our Jersey cow."

GUERNSEY. Origin, Channel Islands. Average weight of cow, 900 pounds. Purpose, butter. Color, an irregular yellow and white, or red and white, or sometimes of solid colors, or nearly so. Coarser in frame and less beautiful than the Jersey, but her equal in percentage of butter fat and her superior in quantity of milk. A gentle cow of highest dairy merit. Shown in colored Plate II.

LEMON-COLORED GUERNSEY BULL.

The Channel Islands cattle, both Guernsey and Jersey, are of the very highest value to the butter maker. They are also in demand among milk producers, being used to "color up" or make yellow the milk of other breeds.

These cattle are built upon the triangle plan—heavy and deep behind and rather light in front; the milking type. They are characterized by yellow skins, the color being particularly noticeable inside the ears. They breed early.

The Channel Islands cattle have been bred pure, it is said, for five hundred years; and it is unlawful to carry any living bull, of any breed, to these islands.

Alderney was a name formerly, but not now, applied to the Channel Islands cattle, especially the Jerseys.

AYRSHIRE. Origin, County of Ayr, Scotland. Weight of cow, 900 pounds. Purpose, dairy. Color, usually red or brown and white, in large patches.

Sometimes all red or brown; sometimes black and white. An old breed. She has been called "the rent-payer."

This cow is hardy. Her admirers claim she will produce a larger quantity of good milk for the food consumed than any other breed. She is classed as a cheese cow rather than as a butter cow, though also a good butter maker. A beautiful Ayrshire is shown in colored Plate III.

AYRSHIRE BULL.

HOLSTEIN-FRIESIAN. Origin, Denmark, Germany, Holland. Weight of cow, 1200 to 1400 pounds. Purpose, milk, cheese; though also used for butter. Color, usually black and white. A noble race. The name is a compromise, now including blood from several former families. The typical Holstein-Friesian is well known. This breed has probably the highest milk record in the world for quantity, and an effort is in progress for the improvement of the quality. A famous Holstein cow is painted in colored Plate IV.

A PRIZE HOLSTEIN.

HEREFORD. Origin, England. Weight of cow, 1200 to 1400 pounds. Purpose, milk, cheese, beef. Color, a distinct red, not too dark; white face, mane, breast and belly; white end to tail, and white legs as high as knee and hock.

This is a breed of great antiquity and recognized merit. The Herefords are good but not deep milkers. As beef makers they are at the top of the market. They are hardy, and well adapted to cold climates. A prize winning cow is shown in colored Plate V.

SHORTHORN. Formerly called Durham. Origin, England. Weight of cow, 1200 to 1600 pounds. Purpose, milk, cheese, beef. Color, roan, white, red, white and red; but not in spots. See the roan type in colored Plate VI.

SHORTHORN BULL.

The breed is comparatively modern, and is in high favor in England and in certain parts of the United States. The Shorthorn is without a rival for beef, and has been bred up to a good milking standard. She is unrivaled for cheese making. When bred strictly for beef the ideal Shorthorn assumes the shape of a parallelogram, from whatever point viewed.

DEVON. Of English origin. Weight of cow (there are two strains in America) 1000 to 1200 pounds. Purpose, milk, beef. Color, a rich dark red.

The milk of the Devon is said to be especially adapted for human food, particularly the food of infants.

"TAURUS," A FAMOUS DEVON.

The Devons are smaller than the Shorthorns and Herefords, but larger than the Ayrshires and Channel

Islands cattle. The udder is comparatively small, and the milk yield usually above what would be expected. The milking period is long. Devon beef has a high reputation. The breed is an old one.

ABERDEEN-ANGUS. Polled Angus, Polled Aberdeen-Angus. A hornless breed, of Scotch origin. Weight of cow, 1300 or 1400 pounds. Purpose, milk, beef. Bred pure for three-quarters of a century. Black.

Considerable numbers have come to the United States, and are now advertised by their breeders. They hold high rank for certain purposes, especially for beef. This breed, when exposed to winter weather, develops an excellent coat that makes a warm carriage robe when properly tanned.

DUTCH BELTED. Origin, Holland. Weight of cow, 1200 pounds. Purpose, dairy products, beef.

A DUTCH BELTED GROUP.

Color, black and white, the white being in a blanket around the body.

This belted stock is beautiful, but its standard of purity appears to be in part a matter of fancy.

GALLOWAY. Of Scotch origin. Weight of cow,

1250 pounds. Purpose, milk and beef. Color, black with brownish tinge. See colored Plate VII.

The Galloways are a polled or hornless breed, especially adapted to cold, exposed countries, as they are very hardy. They are bred in the United States and advertised in the agricultural papers. These hardy animals have thick coats of hair.

RED POLLED. Of English origin. Weight of cow, 1300 or 1400 pounds. Purpose, beef, milk, cheese. Pure bred for a century. Color, a deep red,

THREE YOUNG ONES AND THEIR FATHER.

with udder of the same color; but tip of tail may be white. Nose not dark or cloudy.

This hornless breed was formerly known as Norfolk Polled or Suffolk Polled. The Red Polled cattle are adapted to severe winters, and are growing in favor in the northern and western portions of the United States. The Red Polled cow does not mature as early as the smaller breeds. See colored Plate VIII.

BROWN SWISS. Origin, Switzerland. Weight of cow, 1200 to 1300 pounds. Purpose, dairy products. Color, dun or mouse, fading to gray on back, with a strip of light gray or nearly white along the belly.

There are two varieties of Swiss cattle in the United States, commonly known as the brown and the spotted. The Brown Schwytzer was imported in 1869, and at once made a good record. The Simmenthal (Simmenthaler) or Bernese cow is a larger animal, and differently marked, having irregular and sharply defined spots or bars of red, yellow or drab. This breed has a high repute for usefulness as work oxen, and is an excellent strain for the dairy.

BROWN SWISS COW.

The AMERICAN HOLDERNESS breed (first herd book published in 1880) is said to have wholly descended from an imported bull and cow of Holderness stock from Yorkshire, England.

The best pedigree for the poor man is performance.—John Tucker.

NATIVE. More than nine-tenths of the cows of the United States are so-called natives or scrubs. The latter term is widely used in the West and South; the former is a better name, more applicable to a useful animal.

Our native cow is the product of various European importations. Cattle were brought here in 1609 from the West Indies; in 1625 from Holland; in 1627 from Sweden; in 1631 from Denmark. The old Denmarks were light yellow; the Dutch black and white; the Spanish and Welsh generally black; the Devons red. The latter were the foundation stock in some states. Denmark crossed with Spanish made a dark brindle. Denmark and Devon made a light brindle. The Shorthorn blood enters largely into the native stock in many localities. Of course a mixed ancestry means an uncertain progeny. A valuable native cow may or may not produce a calf of equal merit, but a good thoroughbred bull will make a good calf a reasonable probability.

SCRUBS.

Breed with a purpose—a 5000 pound purpose at least.

A poor butter cow may sometimes be used as a foster mother for calves.

The polled (hornless) bulls are likely to produce hornless calves.

Test the milk before buying the cow.

A good pedigree will not atone for lack of care.

Animals are best imported at the age of one year.

Away with all pensioners, all scrubs, all unprofitable boarders.

A scrub with a pedigree is a worse scrub than the scrub without a pedigree.

Milk quality is said to depend on breed, and milk quantity on feed.

The worst kind of a scrub is a scrub milker.

PLATE 1.

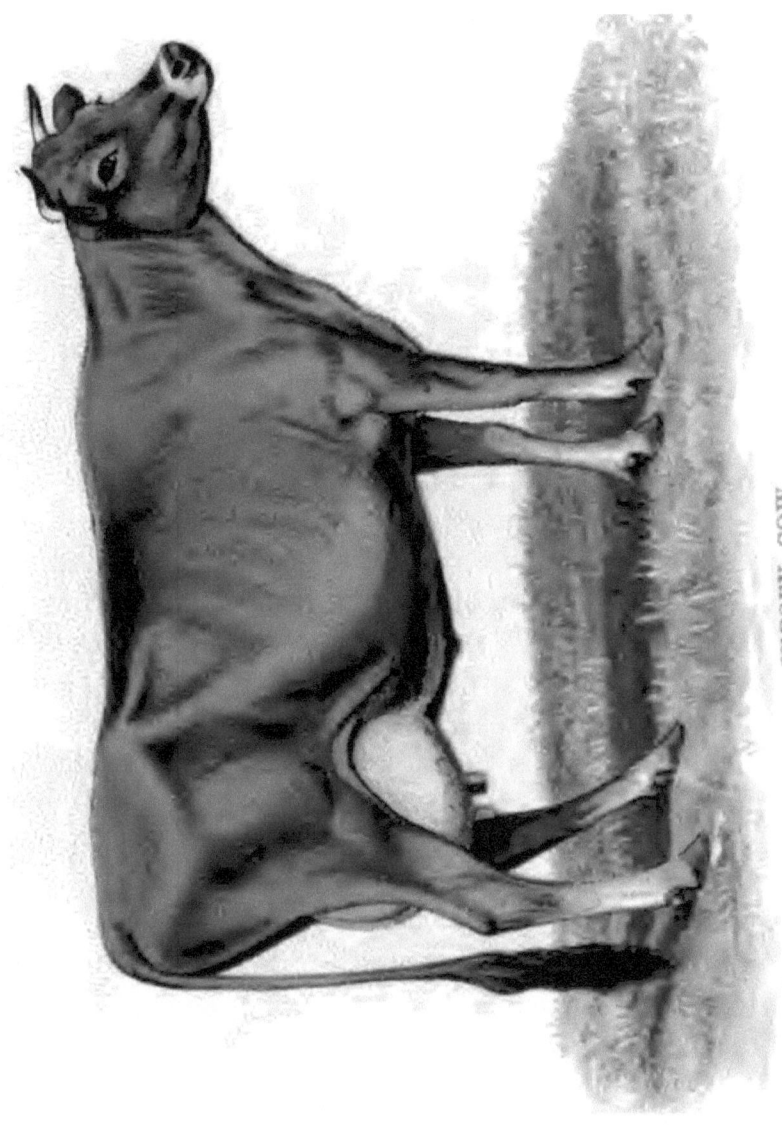

JERSEY COW.

Chapter III.

THE BULL.

The bull is half the herd.—Old Saying.

To raise thoroughbreds is one thing; to breed up a herd of native or grade cattle for dairy purposes or for beef is another thing. To succeed in the latter work requires a distinctly-defined purpose and an unwavering adherence to that purpose.

The first thing is to get a good bull. The next is to know each cow of the herd mathematically; to be certain of her yield in pounds and in butter fat. The removal of the unprofitable cow is a great step in the right direction.

The selection of the bull should begin with the selection of his grandparents. He should be a thoroughbred and the offspring of good milkers.

A heifer head on a bull is not the right sort. A bull should have a bull's head.

The young bull is fit for service at sixteen months, but should be used the first year on not more than a dozen cows. The second year the number of cows may be doubled.

It is far better to keep a really good, thoroughbred bull, and to charge $5 for his use, and thus limit him, than to charge only $1 for more frequent service.

Bulls become dangerous, usually, because of unexpended muscular energy; and light work adds not only to their docility but to their prepotency. Exercise is not merely good for them, but actually necessary for their health, but do not let them run in the pasture with the cows, as most farmers do.

The bull should be stabled apart from the cows with direct access to the service yard or pen. This should be surrounded by a high board fence. Do not keep him in solitary confinement in some dark, dirty pen.

For work or for exercise a so-called one-horse power is a good machine; and the bull's strength may be turned to useful account. Or the animal may be broken to harness, and made to draw a cart. But excessive work is as harmful as excessive idleness. The age limit of usefulness is regulated by health and strength.

HOW IS THIS?

Never trust a bull. It is the harmless bull that generally does harm, as it is the gun not loaded that kills.

DON'T.

Don't pet the bull. Don't trust even a muley.

Don't deny the bull some sort of a gymnasium.

Don't keep the scrub bull out of the beef barrel very long.

Don't expect a bull to regard a fence as strong until he has failed to knock it down.

Don't permit a snapping cur to worry the bull and frighten the cows.

Don't defer dehorning the bull until he has killed somebody (as my neighbor did).

Chapter IV.

MOTHER COW.

The cow is the personality of motherhood. Her owner should never forget this.—John Tucker.

Whether it is better to raise cows or to buy them is an open question. Both plans are practised by successful dairymen. It is thought by some that it is better and cheaper to buy fresh cows from drovers, sell the calves, work the animals at high pressure as long as they yield a given amount of milk, and then sell them for what they will bring, replacing them with fresh cows from the drover.

This plan has many advocates among good dairymen; yet it has many objections in practice.

The other method, that of raising the heifer calves, may or may not be more profitable, but it is certainly more scientific. Buying may demand more wit, but breeding demands more brains.

The cow's period of pregnancy is slightly variable, but 280 days may be given as an average, with a few days additional in case of a male calf. The breeding period occurs at intervals of twenty or twenty-one days.

Service in December or January will produce calves in September or October; and this is a very good time for the winter dairy.

The smaller breeds of cattle arrive at maturity earlier than the larger breeds. Jerseys have been bred at the age of seven months, but ten to fifteen months is better. This brings the heifer into profit at the age of two years. The heavy breeds reach maturity a year later.

During pregnancy the heifer or cow should be well and wisely fed. The quantity must supply two lives; the quality must favor growth and development of the unborn calf, to say nothing of the milk supply. For some time before calving the food supply must be reduced. This is in recognition of the fact that the growth of the calf has been practically completed, that the milk yield is to cease, and that certain great changes are in progress. The nourishment of the fœtus through the umbilical cord is to end, and the production of milk in the mammary glands is to begin.

HER FIRST BORN.

It is well for cows in milk to be dried off a month or six weeks before calving. This is best accomplished by cutting off the supply of milk-producing food and milking only once a day. Hay may be given freely, but not much grain.

The birth of the calf is usually an event involving no especial pain or difficulty to the parent cow, but in the presence of alarming symptoms a veterinarian must be called in. Ordinarily it is safe to trust the whole operation to nature.

Give each cow a box stall at least two weeks before calving, where she can be warm and quiet.

The dam will lick dry her offspring and the calf will usually go to sucking of its own accord. The careful dairyman will, however, try to keep an eye on important events of this character, since accidents sometimes happen.

The first milk of the cow is of a peculiar character. It is especially designed by nature to act as a purgative, and thus put the bowels of the young calf in perfect working condition. The first milk is called colostrum.

It is advised by some dairymen not to milk the cow dry for a few days after calving, because by so doing, you cause an unnatural flow of the milk, and all sorts of complications ensue.

The milk of the cow is generally considered fit for human food four days after the birth of the calf.

A mature cow may safely drop a calf once a year, but a heifer should be allowed a considerable period of rest between the time of dropping her first calf and her next period of gestation. This rest will aid in her growth and maturity and will help to fix upon her character the habit of milk-

HARRIET'S PET.

ing. If the first calf is dropped when the heifer is two years old, let the next be dropped when she is three and a half years old.

Warm water (90°) is advisable for cows immediately after calving. A little bran in the water is often used; or bran may be given separately. The cow should be kept on dry straw, and should be allowed to come to her appetite very gradually. Common sense should be depended on largely during the critical period after calving. Avoid cold water, cold wind, wet bedding, overfeeding. Make the cow comfortable, and watch her bag. If her bowels stubbornly fail to move, Epsom salts must be used. But it is better to have the cow in such good condition that nature will do most of the work.

The term of a cow's usefulness is a thing of fact, not theory. High pressure will exhaust a cow in a few years. Good care will prolong her life. Drove cows are sometimes worn out in three years, while home-bred cows may last three or four times as long.

WEDGE SHAPE.

The accepted type of the milk cow is the wedge; that is, deep behind, with light shoulders and head.

The accepted type of the beef cow is the parallelogram; that is, the "brick-set-on-edge" form.

It must be borne in mind that each and every type of cow may be the best; no dairyman can judge for another dairyman.

BRICK-SET-ON-EDGE TYPE.

Then, again, there are individual cows which differ in their products widely from the generally accepted family type, as certain Jerseys which produce a great volume of milk and certain Holsteins which produce a heavy yield of butter. It shows the possible power of the breeder over the animal. The important thing is to breed persistently for a definite purpose.

The external cow is worthy of study as typical of merit or demerit. The head should be comparatively small and limbs slender. The neck should be rather long, in harmony with the idea of good grazing qualities. The back should be straight, eyes prominent and bright, belly large and deep, tail slender, udder large, teats large and set well apart, milk vein prominent, hair soft, and skin pliable. It is natural to expect a yellow skin inside the ear and on the extreme tip of the tail in all cows giving richly-colored milk. The color of the horns is not essential.

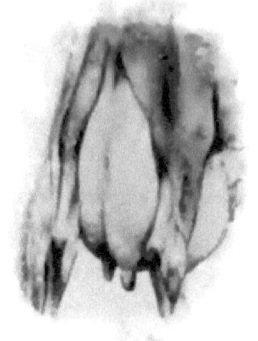

A WELL-SET UDDER.

The internal cow is no matter of fancy or fashion. She must have good teeth, good stomachs and a good udder. She may be a milk producer or a beef producer or a combination of the two; but without digestive ability she is next to nothing.

There was a theory quite widely promulgated a few years ago and not yet obsolete for judging the value of dairy cows by the so-called escutcheon or milk-mirror. It is called the Guenon theory. It depends upon a view of the rear of the udder and adjacent parts. A perfect escutcheon, indicative of a high grade dairy cow, demands a large udder to begin with, accom-

ESCUTCHEON OF A GOOD BUTTER BULL.

panied by certain growth and arrangement of the adjacent hair on the flanks.

That there is something in the Guenon theory need not be denied; but if so good an authority as Governor Hoard says that it is of no practical use to him it is scarcely worth while to expect much of it in ordinary dairying.

Dehorning cattle is now more or less widely practised in the United States, and there are several hornless breeds getting a wide foothold in the country.

NO HORNS HERE.

Horns may be bred off altogether, after a time. It seems to be feasible to produce polled cattle of any desired type.

Every dairy should have a milk standard, and every cow should come up to the standard or get out of the herd. A yearly product of 5000 pounds of milk is low enough; 6000 or 7000 pounds is better.

Remember the old saying about the profits being in the top of the pail.

COWSLIPS.

The cow is not a race horse.

Treat the nervous cow gently.

A low voice makes a quiet cow.

Do not water the cow in the icy creek.

If 'tis currycomb for horse it should be currycomb for cow.

A barbed-wire fence is a poor December wind-break for cows.

Old advice but excellent: Speak to a cow as you would to a lady.

More "Come, bossy," and less "Get around there," will fill the pail.

The barking dog and the cow's heels should be kept wide apart.

Let the cows pasture at night in fly-time; stable them in the daytime.

The cow in heat should not be turned in the same pasture with the others.

In buying a dairy cow from a dairyman, it is safe not to take the seller's pick.

If the stable is cold at calving time blanket the cow after the birth of the calf, and the calf too.

A cow's milk should amount each year to five times her own weight. Do not be contented with less.

Which way does the hair stand on your cows? A cow that has to work for her food will return no profit.

A carefully made test proves that in some cases excitement robs the milk of more than one-half its butter.

Count no cow handsome that does not daily produce at least a one-pound print. Many cows are making two.

It is a foolish notion to stint the rations of a dry cow. She needs to build up after a period of generous milking.

Remember that bacteria swarm in the cellar as well as in the cow stable. A careless housekeeper is as blamable as a careless dairyman.

Fat globules are small—millions to the quart. But do not be frightened; they are weighed, not counted. Be sure to have at least 4½ pounds of them in every 100 pounds of milk.

> "The friendly cow all red and white,
>   I love with all my heart;
> She gives me cream with all her might
>   To eat with apple-tart."

THE HAPPY DAYS OF YOUTH.

Chapter V.

BABY.

Too much is expected of a calf a day old; it does not know much; how could it?—Harriet.

True is it that if the calf is not fed suitable food and regularly it will not do its best. And if it fail to do its best as a calf its usefulness when mature will be impaired. The best food for the calf is new milk, nature's own provision. When beginning life it needs a peculiar physic, gradually lessening in intensity the first few days. This the new-milch cow supplies, and it should be given the new calf, always.

To teach the Baby to drink is easier than many suppose. A small quantity of milk and a large supply of patience and perseverance mixed are the requisites. Take a quart of milk in an eight or ten quart pail, give it two of your fingers to suck air between, and by degrees lower its nose into the pail, for by nature it points it skyward. After it finds it can draw milk instead of air between the fingers it will not be long in relaxing its neck muscles. After a little it may be weaned from the fingers. If it will not drink at first it must be left for a few hours to increase its appetite.

CALF FEEDER.

If new milk cannot be spared after three days, skimmilk may be substituted, but this must be done judiciously, particularly at first. A sudden change from new milk to a substitute must not be made. A half-pint of skimmilk must be put in the mess, and day by day it must be increased until skimmilk is fed entirely. It is well also to change the calf from sweet

FEEDING THE CALVES.

to sour milk, particularly if it is to be reared during hot weather when it is not always possible to keep the milk sweet. Calves fed on sour milk do as well as those reared on sweet milk, and run no risk of several of the diseases incident to calfhood. Changing from one to the other is a fertile source of trouble.

Good calves may be raised on buttermilk alone, but they should not run to grass while living upon it, hay being kept by them, thus avoiding the prevalence of scours. It is best to give calves some liquid food from the pail, for at least three months. Besides this they should learn to eat as soon as possible, when a little middlings in a shallow trough may be given daily, together with other food.

Where it is not convenient to get milk to raise a calf it may be brought up successfully on hay tea. Boil cut clover hay in water until its strength is extracted. Wean the calf from milk to this tea precisely as if it were skimmilk. Whatever the food, however, remember there is more danger in overfeeding than in underfeeding. Too much is usually the cause of that enemy of the calf, scours or diarrhœa, as a remedy for which nothing equals starvation. But prevention is far better than cure; and never lose sight of the axiom that a growing animal should never be allowed to stop growth until matured in the most thorough manner. Never fatten a young animal you expect to raise.

To make veal in the simplest manner is to let the calf suck or to feed the warm or new milk five to eight weeks. But this is also the most expensive way. To sell butter fats and at the same time sell veal requires a stroke of genius, but some are doing it to their great profit and satisfaction. A calf must be a prodigy to pay fifteen to twenty cents per pound for butter fats, and only rich men can afford to feed such expensive foods.

A LITTLE SHAKY YET.

A common practice is to replace cream with flaxseed jelly; that is to feed calves with skimmilk to which flaxseed jelly has been added. Of the jelly use half a teacupful in the milk at each meal, increasing it slowly until a pint is fed in the skimmilk twice per day. To make the jelly, boil one pound of whole flaxseed in water until a thick paste results. It needs no straining, and only to be kept cold while it lasts. Some have good results by carefully using corn meal or oat meal instead of the flaxseed.

When feeding grain to calves in connection with skimmilk, a little point worth remembering is to put the grain in the pail after pouring in the milk. It seems to mix better with the milk than if put in the bottom of the pail and the milk poured on top of it.

The most profitable veal is made in four to five weeks, every added day after this increasing the cost per pound rapidly.

Fall calves have a distinct advantage over calves beginning life in the spring. Given warm, clean quarters and better care than the hurry of the summer will permit, they become strong and their digestion lusty before the season when flies annoy and the sun becomes too hot for comfort. Such calves dropped in the early fall and given the right of way all winter resemble, in the spring, yearlings dropped the previous spring.

CALF WISDOM.

Skimmilk has nearly all the protein of the new milk; and protein is the muscle and tissue builder.

Good calves are real mortgage lifters.

Feed no mouldy hay or grain to calves.

Coax the calves; make pets of them.

Teach the calf to lead.

Keep the baby dry.

SHELTER FOR CALVES.

The new calf will begin to eat hay at a week old. You couldn't do it.

The infant should be a little hungry three times a day.

Keep the young calves in pens separate from the older ones.

GUERNSEY COW.

Chapter VI.

THE HEIFER.

You can grow a better cow during the first two years of a calf's life than in all the time after that.—Tim.

It is quite as important to feed a well-balanced ration to a heifer as to a cow in milk. A balanced ration is not a theory but a way of making every food unit count for the utmost. About 1:4.8 is right for the heifer; rich in protein because the animal is forming tissue rapidly.

You can't win a heifer without wooing her; and unless she confides in you there is trouble ahead. Pet her every day now, and you will gain time and milk and save vexation when she calves.

Be careful not to dry the young cows in milk when stabling them for the winter. Milk them clean, pamper their appetites and be good to them. If they will milk right through to calving, all the better. A heifer easily learns to dry off early, and will ever after remember the trick. When mature she will be profitable eleven months in the year, when she might be kept at a loss if dry three to five months.

The wrinkles grow on the horns of cattle when they are going on three years of age, and when three years old there is generally one well defined wrinkle around the horns close to the head. The next year there are two, and one additional every year. These wrinkles denote the age, counting the first one three.

A PRETTY PARTY.

When calves are born in the autumn and stunted, the wrinkles get out of order and are not reliable as to age. On well raised calves the rule is about certain.

FRISKIES.

To scratch a nervous heifer between her fore legs has a wonderfully soothing effect.

A cow well broken to the halter, and gentle, is worth much more than one that is unmanageable.

Do not permit heifers to be worried, alarmed or annoyed.

Heifers are timid. They need reassurance.

The well-fed, well-stabled, well-trained heifer literally grows into money.

Have heifers that are worth raising, and then treat them accordingly.

The heifer becomes a cow at two years of age, and is then self-supporting.

Chapter VII.

THE OX.

There is no richer autumn picture than an ox-cart loaded with golden corn.—Harriet.

Let us train the steers; go at it gently, one at a time. August is a good time to select or match up steers and to train them. Any odd times when work is not pressing may thus be made profitable. Put him on the barn floor if you have no other place. Take a whip with a long stock and a short lash and stand in the middle of the floor and drive the steer around you. Never strike him a hard blow. Tell him to go on, and let him go on till he goes around well. Then teach him to stop at the word *whoa*.

When the word is given touch him on the forehead with the whip rapidly until he stops; then brush him a little and give him a nubbin of corn. Kindness goes a great ways. Keep him from getting excited. You can do nothing with a crazy steer. Give one lesson a day to each steer.

The second day teach him to *haw*. This is done by first stopping him as before, and then gently tapping him on the off hip. Reverse this training

A FAMOUS YOKE. "JOE" AND "JERRY." TOTAL WEIGHT 7300 LBS.

to *gee* and walk around his head to turn him. After each steer, by itself, has learned these rudiments of its education, then put them both together in the yoke in the same place and do not let them run, but walk around together. Teach them to stop together at the word, to *haw* and *gee*, and back up. This lesson should be taught singly and a day taken for it. Some people try to teach a steer everything in one day, and then make them used to the yoke, and make runaways of them at the same time, by putting the yoke on them and letting them run. When thus broken oxen can never be depended upon. They will get excited easily and away they will go pell-mell and nothing can stop them.

GADS.

Older than the Pyramids is the use of the ox.

The ox, though not swift, is pretty sure.

The man who has never used a good yoke of oxen has never fully enjoyed farm life.

Little yokes for little oxen; big yokes for big oxen.

If the oxen are the least bit thin feed them up well before plowing time. It will pay.

Do you notice how well good Devon steers sell when well broken?

Shoes are indispensable to oxen during icy terms, and are profitable insurance against accident.

Abandon the barbarous ox-yoke and use a harness like the accompanying cut.  The patient ox will be more useful and will do much more work in this humane outfit, and be free from galls and sores.

Chapter VIII.

FOOD AND DRINK.

Profits are near the top of the milk pail—Dorothy Tucker.

A GOOD MILK MACHINE.

Water cows after feeding.

Feed regularly what each cow will eat up clean, always giving the heaviest feeding at night.

It is easier to keep a cow in a profitable condition, than to get her back to it if allowed to run down.

Do not let the cows eat horse manure; it will make the butter bitter.

A little linseed meal keeps the intestines of all stock open, and they thrive better as a result.

The cow's stomach is a mighty poor filter for filthy water.

No single food is calculated for a complete butter food. Clover hay comes the nearest to a complete butter food.

This chapter is on food and drink, but it should be understood at the outset that big results are impossible with poor cows. There must be a high standard of productive ability and the pensioners must go. There must be a thoroughbred bull or the dairy will not increase in output from year to year, but will remain stationary, or will retrograde.

The American dairyman is blessed with a long list of available cattle foods, but his best policy is always to use his home products as a feeding basis, buying only what is necessary to balance the ration.

The phrases nutritive ratio, well balanced ration, etc., are not hard to understand for those who try.

The agricultural chemist has learned that the tissue-producing elements of the food must bear a certain proportion to the energy and heat-producing elements of the food. This proportion is called the nutritive ratio. It should be as one to five and one-half, or one to six, varying with age, etc. Destroy or ignore this proportion and there is a loss of money, and good food goes to the dung pile, undigested and wasted.

Speaking technically, the elements in cattle feeds are protein, carbohydrates, fats, fibre, ash, water, etc. We are concerned with the first three; and the digestible protein must be in the proportion of one to five, or one to six, as compared with the sum of the digestible carbohydrates and fats. The dairyman need not concern himself about fibre, ash, water, etc. They are always present.

Protein is a name applied to a group of nitrogenous substances. It furnishes, in brief, the material for tissue building. It enters largely into the muscles, blood, milk, tendons, nerves, skin, hair, wool It also has some heat-producing power, but it is mainly a maker of tissue.

The carbohydrates (sugars, starches, gums) and the fats have to do with building up the fat of animals, and are necessary for the production of heat and the maintenance of energy and motion. Their heat-producing power is measured in calories. A calory is the amount of heat required to raise the temperature of a pound of water four degrees Fahrenheit.

The protein makes the engine and the boiler; the carbohydrates and fat are the fuel.

Fat is reckoned to be worth two and one-quarter times the carbohydrates in ability to produce heat and motive power within the body.

Nutritive ratio is merely the proportion of protein to carbohydrates plus fat; the fat being multiplied by two and one-quarter and added to the carbohydrates.

Tables of the digestible ingredients of all feeding stuffs are now published by the Government and by most of the stations, and can be had free of cost. Every dairyman should have such tables at hand for frequent reference. It is not hard to learn to use them.

American dairy practice differs slightly from European practice, but it is believed that the latter (the German standard of Wolff) is more nearly correct. Here are two standards, each intended to represent the daily food of a cow weighing 1000 pounds.

	Total Organic Matter	Digestible Protein	Digestible Carbohydrates	Digestible Fat	Fuel Value (Calories)
German (Wolff's)	24 lbs.	2.50 lbs.	12.50 lbs.	.40 lbs.	29,590
Wisconsin	24.51 lbs.	2.15 lbs.	13.27 lbs.	.74 lbs.	31,250

The first standard is based upon experience and science. The second (Wisconsin) merely represents the average practice of 128 successful American dairymen. The German standard ratio is written 1: 5.4. The Wisconsin standard ratio is 1: 6.9, and is regarded as a little too wide; that is, rather excessive in carbohydrates; not quite enough protein. When the protein is in excess the ration is said to be too narrow.

Dairymen need not use technical terms, but it is obvious that they must know what a good ration really is, and why it is good.

Of course either of the above rations must be increased or decreased in weight as the animal weighs more or less than 1000 pounds.

Dairymen about to make up rations must take full account of home-grown products. Whatever the farm produces best and cheapest must be made the basis of the dairy ration. It may be necessary to buy something to effect a "balance," but the necessity for outside purchases is decreasing as dairymen better understand what the ration really demands and what the farm may supply. Protein is the article in which the coarse fodders are generally deficient, and protein is the most expensive thing to buy. It is usually bought in linseed meal, gluten meal, cottonseed meal, bran, etc.; and yet it can be easily grown at home in the form of peas, soja beans, vetches, tares, clovers, etc. Protein is nitrogen in combination.

BACK FROM THE DAIRY SCHOOL.

An almost perfectly balanced ration can be made of these plants, in the form of hay, and if fed with a small amount of grain for the sake of palatability they can be made to save part of the cost of going to mill.

The following standards are the best now accessible to American dairymen. Balanced rations can easily be made corresponding with them. The total weight of ration is important, and must correspond with weight of animal; the weight of protein is important; but the carbohydrates and fats may be varied slightly, provided their sum total (with fat multiplied by two and one-quarter) be about five and a half times the weight of protein, since carbohydrates and fat serve substantially the same purpose in the food.

In working with tables, in making up rations, it is necessary to observe the terms "dry matter," "digestible protein," "digestible carbohydrates," "digestible fat;" for these terms are intended in the Wolff standard. (The total weight of a cow's ration of twenty-four pounds of dry matter varies greatly. The dry matter in 100 pounds of ensilage amounts to only about twenty pounds, while in 100 pounds of good hay the dry matter amounts to nearly ninety pounds.)

Wolff's (German) Feeding Standards per Day	Average Live Weight per Head	Total (water free) Organic Matter	Digestible Food Materials			Fuel value (Calories)	Nutritive Ratio
			Protein	Carbo-hydrates	Fat		
	lbs.	lbs.	lbs.	lbs.	lbs.		
Milk Cows	1000	24.0	2.5	12.5	.40	29,590	1: 5.4
Growing Cattle, 2 to 3 mos.	150	3.3	0.6	2.1	.30	5,116	1: 4.6
" " 3 to 6 mos.	300	7.0	1.0	4.1	.30	10,750	1: 4.8
" " 6 to 12 mos.	500	12.0	1.3	6.8	.30	16,332	1: 5.8
" " 12 to 18 mos.	700	16.8	1.4	9.1	.28	20,712	1: 6.9
" " 18 to 24 mos	850	20.4	1.4	10.3	.26	22,859	1: 7.8
Fattening Steers, 1st period,	1000	27.0	2.5	15.0	.50	34,660	1: 6.4
" " 2d period,	1000	26.0	3.0	14.8	.70	36,062	1: 5.5
" " 3d period,	1000	25.0	2.7	14.8	.60	35,082	1: 6.0
Oxen moderately worked	1000	24.0	1.6	11.3	.30	24,260	1: 7.4

NOTE.—Weight of ration up to 1000 pounds is actual; above 1000 pounds the weight of ration must be proportionably increased. It will be noticed that the ratio of protein to carbohydrates and fats changes under different conditions, ages, etc.

To show the makeup of a good dairy ration (for a cow weighing 1000 pounds), and to point out the difference between actual weight and "total dry matter," a single example may be given. Any dairyman can adapt a ration to his individual needs. It is an easy, pleasant and profitable pastime. The printed tables, as already stated, can be had free of cost from the nearest experiment station or from the Agricultural Department at Washington.

Ration for Dairy Cows	Total Dry Matter lbs.	Digestible Protein lbs.	Digestible Carbohydrates lbs.	Digestible Fat lbs.	Fuel Value (Calories)
12 pounds clover hay	10.16	.79	4.24	.20	10,199
20 pounds corn silage	4.18	.11	2.36	.13	5,143
4 pounds corn meal	3.40	.28	2.61	.13	5,921
4 pounds wheat bran	3.54	.48	1.65	.11	4,446
4 pounds gluten meal	3.69	.82	1.75	.34	6,223
Total	24.97	2.48	12.61	.91	31,932
Wolff's Standard	24.00	2.50	12.50	.40	29,590

This ration is not offered as a model of economy. In some locations it would be excellent; in other places it would be too expensive. It shows the proper weight of dry matter and nearly the proper proportion of protein to carbohydrates and fat for a cow in milk. The nutritive ratio is about 1:5.9, which is a trifle too wide. Still, it would be a good ration.

As to feeding stuffs (aside from natural pasture) the American range is very large. The green fodders embrace the whole list of grasses, sorghums, millets and leguminous plants. The latter group (including clovers, peas, beans, vetches, tares) is destined to play an important part in dairying, as well as in green manuring, on account of their wonderful ability to take nitrogen from the atmosphere. They are adapted to silage as well as to soiling purposes. Ambitious American dairymen would do well to give full attention to the leguminous plants, as there is money in them both as soil enrichers and as economic stock foods.

Corn fodder, both green and dry, is of great economic importance to dairymen. It adds necessary bulk to the ration, whether used dry or in the form of ensilage. There are various good implements on the market for cutting and shredding dry fodder, to make it more available for stock feeding purposes.

Ensilage and root crops are briefly treated in other chapters. The former has become essential, even in comparatively small dairies. The latter source of succulent food is worthy of increased attention; especially carrots, mangels and sugar beets.

Grain is sometimes, not always, too expensive to feed to dairy cattle. Wheat occasionally drops in price to a point where it can be fed to advantage. Oats is an excellent cow food, when ground and used as a component of a ration. Corn fed whole is largely wasted; and, indeed, it is often wasted when fed in the form of meal in a poorly balanced ration. It is a heat-producer rather than a milk maker. When the starch has been taken out, making gluten meal of it, it is quite a different article, as it is less heating, and has a higher percentage of protein.

CONTENTMENT.

Chapter IX.

FOOD AND DRINK—*Continued*.

You can lead a cow to water, but the other cows may keep her from drinking.—John Tucker.

A word as to the drink of the dairy cow, after which I will return to the food question.

Careful experiments show that cows will sometimes drink as much as seventy-five to one hundred and fifty pounds of water per day if they have free access to it. The average cow will perhaps drink ninety pounds, or say nearly enough to fill a forty quart can every day.

To cut off the water supply is to cut off the milk supply; and everybody knows how the master cows intimidate the weaklings, and sometimes frighten them away from the drinking trough.

The arguments are good for having water within reach of every cow as she stands in her stall. In this way the timid animal is sure to get her fill.

The cow's drinking water must be perfectly pure and preferably cool; cool enough to be palatable and pure because much of the drink goes direct to the milk pail. This is the legitimate way of watering milk. Eighty-seven per cent. of milk being water, let it be good water.

The judgment of a cow as to pure drinking water is not to be trusted.

Returning to the subject of foods, I must speak of ensilage, a thing now indispensable in profitable dairying, on account of excellence and cheapness.

Corn is the main ensilage crop in America. It gains nothing by going through the silo, but neither does it lose anything, and herein lies the profit. The corn-stalks may perhaps gain somewhat in digestibility; but the great end secured is a permanent supply of succulent food. It is as though the farmer could bring to his cows freshly-grown corn-stalks all winter.

The daily amount for a dairy cow is one cubic foot of settled silage, weighing thirty-five to forty pounds. Some feeders use fifty pounds, but a cubic foot is probably quite enough.

On this basis it is easy to figure out the size of a contemplated silo. The cows will be stall-fed for say 200 days. It is therefore necessary to multiply 200 cubic feet by the number of cows in the herd to learn the requisite size of the silo. Or, stated in other terms, an allowance may be made of four tons of silage per cow per year.

A good wooden silo (perfectly round) can be erected at an estimated cost of $1.25 to $2 per ton capacity. The cost of ensilage will of course vary, but $1.50 per ton may be quoted as an average.

ROUND SILO.

Three tons of ensilage are approximately equal in carbohydrates and fat to a ton of red clover hay; but the protein is deficient, and must be supplied in the form of bran or some other nitrogen-bearing food.

Ensilage should be fed gradually at first, and afterward only as part of a well-balanced ration. When intelligently fed it is one of the most excellent and economical foods within reach of the practical dairyman.

Future dairying will no doubt involve the use of peas, beans and other leguminous plants for silage, on account of the high percentage of protein which they contain. Leading stock feeders are aware of the economic value of these plants, and are beginning to use them in ration making.

Of the many commercial articles available for balancing cattle rations and supplying protein (in which ensilage and the coarse fodders are usually deficient) the more common are linseed or cake meal, cottonseed meal, gluten, glucose, brewers' grains, wheat bran, wheat shorts, etc.

These mill feeds are produced in such great numbers, and under so many names, that it is impossible for me even to enumerate them in this little book. The proper thing for a stock feeder to do is to get the tabulated bulletins of the stations, and study the ingredients of these foods in connection with their commercial cost.

The nutritive ratio of potatoes is about 1 : 12. A good cow food can be made by the addition of cottonseed meal, bran, or other protein-bearing ingredient. The advisability of feeding potatoes is largely a question of economy, depending on market price.

Cottonseed meal, a by-product of the manufacture of cottonseed oil, is very rich in protein.

Linseed meal, old process, is the by-product of removing the oil of flaxseed by pressure. Linseed meal, new process, is the result of removing the oil by solvents. The latter contains a higher percentage of protein.

As to cooking or steaming food for cattle, there is little to recommend the practice except in case of fodders where the palatability is increased by the operation.

It is good practice, however, to cut hay and fodder, and sprinkle meal over it, and moisten with water, and then mix thoroughly in a trough prepared for the purpose. This makes a large bulk of palatable and nutritious material.

And do not forget the salt.

Yet, after all, June pasturage is the ideal cow food. It possesses succulence, volume, nutrition. The nutritive ratio of Kentucky blue grass (green grass) is about 1:7, and of red clover about 1:5. Together they make rich pasturage.

SHORT PASTURE.

The ration fed in the stable may be made as palatable, as succulent, and as productive of milk as the best pasture of early summer.

When no pasture can be provided for the calves, they can be picketed so as to have plenty of feed without too cumbersome a rope, by having two picket pins joined by a smooth wire, to which by means of a swivel is attached the calf's rope so that it will slip on the wire. When new grass is necessary move the picket pins alternately. The length of the wire will determine the size of the grazing space.

A FEW ANALYSES.

Dry Matter and Digestible Food Ingredients in 100 pounds.

	Dry Matter lbs.	Protein lbs.	Carbohydrates lbs.	Fat lbs.	Fuel Value
Wheat bran	88.5	12.01	41.23	2.87	111,138
Corn meal	85.0	7.01	65.20	3.25	148,026
Oats	89.0	9.25	48.34	4.18	124,757
Gluten meal	91.2	25.49	42.32	10.38	169,930
Hominy chops	88.9	7.45	55.24	6.81	145,342
Malt sprouts	89.8	18.72	43.50	1.16	120,624
Brewers' grains (dry)	91.1	14.73	36.60	4.82	115,814
Cottonseed meal	91.8	37.01	16.52	12.58	152,653
Linseed meal, n. p.	89.8	27.89	36.36	2.73	131,026
Clover hay	84.7	6.58	35.35	1.66	84,995
Timothy hay	86.8	2.89	43.72	1.43	92,729
Mixed hay	87.1	4.22	43.26	1.33	93,925
Ensilage (corn)	20.9	.56	11.79	.65	25,714
Corn fodder	57.8	2.48	33.38	1.15	71,554
Potatoes	21.1	1.27	15.59	—	31,360
Beets	13.0	1.21	8.84	.05	18,904
Turnips	9.5	.81	6.46	.11	13,986
Mangels	9.1	1.03	5.65	.11	12,888

MIXED FEED.

Well-cured clover hay and some good yellow carrots—nothing better for coloring butter.

Make a balanced ration (as near as may be) from home-grown products. Cut down the bill for mill feed.

Clover hay is the dairyman's mainstay.

Chopped apples and bran; try them.

Feed most what you can grow best.

All radical food changes must be made gradually.

Eight or ten cows will warrant a silo; preferably a round one.

The best cows drink the most; washy foods make washy milk.

Many a so-so cow can be made extra good with more food.

Never turn the stock out the first time when the grass is wet. It may cause hoven or bloat.

A yell stops digestion and secretion.

> "Where the bubbling water flows
> As it through the meadow goes,
> Where the grass is fresh and fine,
> Pretty cow, go there and dine."

A CHESTER COUNTY STOCK BARN.

Chapter X.

THE BARN.

People who winter their cows out of doors on straw or poor hay, are the ones who complain of hollow horn, and make this the excuse for the wretched condition of their cattle. Got the hollow horn! It would be the truth to say, got the hollow belly.—John Tucker.

The location and construction of farm buildings always depend so greatly upon conditions that there can be no arbitrary rules. If the side of a hill with south or east exposure can be secured, a gravity barn may be built that will greatly save time and facilitate the doing of chores. Occasionally a barn is made with driveway into the gable, and thus all the hay and silage are pitched down into bay or silo and down into stable, the manure also going down into the cellar on cart placed there. For storage barns the modern tendency is for buildings of great height, to utilize as much space as possible under small roof area, and to build stock barns but one story to gain more light and better ventilation.

To use the horse fork, which is a great time and labor saver in barns on level ground, all cross works should be avoided by the truss system shown in *Fig. 1*. This brings but trifling increase of cost and greater strength. With a barn built so, the mows may be laid out where one desires, and when empty the floor is clear from end to end. A silo

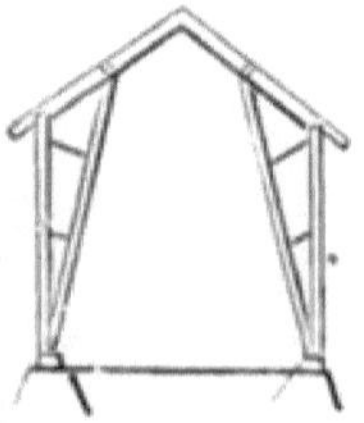

FIG. 1.

could be put in at one end if desired. The building shown herewith illustrates an ingenious adaptation of an old plan to modern requirements. Erected with basement to the yard, as was very common formerly, the basement to serve for stabling or manure, a cow stable of ten feet posts has been placed in the yard. This permits the little door at the end of the store barn floor to be used as a chute, through which the hay and stalks are passed to the cement floor of the new stable. Then if that modern necessity in profitable dairying, the silo, be adopted, and it is thought best to place it in a part of the discarded basement, the ensilage is handed into the stable very easily on car or barrow.

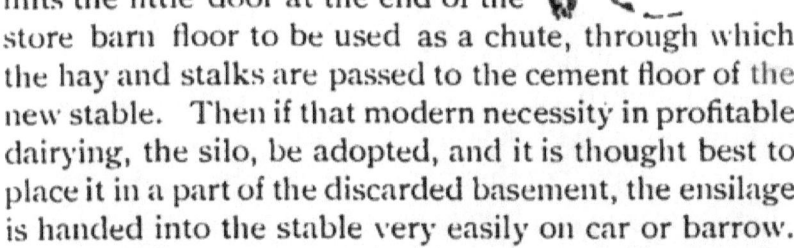

The plank barn is becoming very popular in parts of the west. It is made entirely without heavy timbers, plank being spiked or bolted together to make the varying thicknesses required. It is made to break joints carefully, and any length of beam or truss is thus secured. Such timbers are easily shaped and prove superior in strength to solid beams. Roofs nearly oval or dome shape, and of great strength, may be made that render a barn remarkably capacious. What applies to barns is true also for silos. This principle in building doubtless has a great future.

This is a single illustration of several styles of bents of plank barns. The outer, stack-like shape is made of plank and supports the girts, to which the covering is nailed. The other work is made in the same way of planks of more or less thicknesses, these bolted together to form powerful trusses at each bent.

In many barns now existing the stalls for the cattle are allowed too little space, or more properly the stalls cut into space that ought to be left behind the cattle for a manure ditch and a raised walk. The illustration shows how such a difficulty may be remedied where existing, and how new barns may economize space—a desirable feature. The cattles' standing floor is moved forward to the edge of the feeding floor, with a solid partition between. A part of this partition is arranged, however, to open down on hinges and be held by a chain, to form a crib for the cattle, upright poles being arranged to hold the hay from slipping down under their feet, but far enough apart to allow the cattle to feed through them. All that is required is that they may be able to get their noses through, as the hay will keep constantly slipping toward them as eaten. When the feed is eaten, and at night in particular, this crib can be shut up out of the way, making the stalls very warm indeed. For feeding grain, ensilage or roots a feed box is provided that slips through the partition in front of each animal, and is removed when empty. A feed box should be provided for each stall. The boxes can then be gathered, filled and wheeled on a truck or barrow to the cribs.

Manure is worthy of good care. One of the best cheap shelters is shown in the sketch. It is a lean-to by the side of the barn built wide enough to back the wagons into or drive through for loading when hauling out manure. Or it may shelter carts into which the stable clearing is done direct, thus saving one handling. Outside drop-boarding will be noticed. This is in ten feet sections, hinged at *A*, and is to keep out cold from the barn at night and let in light by day as well as to ventilate the manure. A drain may run from the stable into this manure storage room there to be absorbed.

Here is a good plan for the floor of stall. The dotted portion represents the cement, while the rest is of wood. It will be seen that the fore feet of the cattle stand upon plank, laid cross-wise to keep the cattle from slipping when reaching for their fodder. An unbroken surface of cement extends from this back over the platform, down about the inside of the manure gutter and up to the floor of the walk. This projects over the cement to protect the edge of the latter.

In constructing the manure gutter it should be placed nearer the feed-box or trough at one end of the row of stalls than the other, to accommodate cows of different lengths, and the stalls will vary in width from four and one-half to five and one-half feet.

A cement floor for the cow stable is durable, easily cleaned and cheapest eventually. How to lay it is no secret, but many go wrong, lacking the knowledge. First buy the best cement—Portland, although it costs most, goes three times as far as the same money in cheap cement. To one barrel of Portland use eight barrels of gravel or sand and broken stone, measuring and not guessing. Then mix thoroughly, three times, before wetting. Pour on no water but sprinkle with a watering-pot as the third mixing is being done. Only moisten, don't wet it. Have it just so it will retain its shape when a little is pressed in the hand. Have the foundation ready in advance. If you can get stone stand it on edge six inches deep and pound it all hard. Or use six inches of gravel tamped solid. Then set up edge pieces to lay a strip three to four feet wide and pour in the concrete four inches, two inches at a time, tramping it solid each time. On top make a surface of cement half inch thick; cement one part, sand (screened) two parts. Each layer must dry slowly.

One of the useful things on the stock farm is an elevated walk from the barn floor out over the feed yard. A row of racks is made beneath the walk. The hay is easily carried a forkful at a time and dropped into these racks, from which it is eaten by the cattle in the sun at noonday.

COMFORTABLES.

Cows need much water, but not in the form of cold autumn rains.

Do not turn cows out in a cold wind for exercise. The animal heat is wasted.

No live stock more than cows better appreciate dry bedding.

A hole in the stable is a hole in the pocket.

Thirty-cent butter is too costly to use for filling the cracks in the walls of the cow stable.

Gilt-edged butter cannot be made when the cows are kept in a dark, foul smelling, poorly ventilated stable.

While we must wake up and get the out-door idea out of our head, we ought not keep the cows too closely confined or too warm. A happy medium in this matter is required.

A GOOD HALF OF THE HERD.

Chapter XI.

STABLE REQUISITES.

To save steps is to save men and wages.—Tim.

The ideal stall has a floor level, or nearly level. The cow may be fastened with a chain or with the Newton tie. I do not like stanchions. It is desirable to have but little forward and backward freedom of motion lest the droppings foul the cow's hinder parts, including the udder, when she lies down.

A useful device for adding to the comfort of the cow and the cleanliness of her products is the curry comb. Do not forget it, please. If there is horse food in a curry comb there is also cow food. A clean skin and brisk circulation of blood is quite as essential in the milker as in the trotter.

Drinking troughs or tanks in front of every stall, or every other stall, are to be recommended. They pay.

A trough or tub of water standing all day under the rays of the summer sun, becomes very unpalatable for cattle. An automatic arrangement for keeping water cool is shown in the cut. A loose cover is suspended over the trough by ropes. Cattle and horses will quickly learn to press this aside and drink, when the cover will come back over the water again. Make the cover light and support it evenly as shown.

The cattle should not be allowed to drink ice cold

water. A trough may be hung on a pivot, just above the centre as shown here, so that upon a cold day the water can be dumped out after the stock are watered.

Where ground feed is given to stock much labor and time are wasted unless it is all prepared at once and all fed out of the same receptacle. A handy barrow for this purpose is shown herewith. It is water-tight so that all the feed can be mixed in it, wheeled along in front of the stock and each one given its ration.

A good milking stool has a seat and a table for the pail to rest on. It is eighteen inches long, ten inches wide and thirteen inches in height, as shown here.

One of the requisites aside from clean udders and cleanly milkers is a good milk strainer.

There is need for some kind of a power and some kind of a cutter or shredder on every dairy farm. There is less waste of coarse stuff when cut than when uncut. It can be flavored with meal, and the cows will consume a great deal more of it when thus prepared. Besides, the ration can be better controlled, better weighed, and better balanced where the cutter is used. A mixing trough, where cut hay and fodder can be mixed with meal and moisture, has a place in all large cow stables.

A feeding stand for calves is handy for the pen or field, or any place where it is desired to feed grain to them. The stand is fourteen inches high made of inch pine, with a crosspiece of hard wood and legs of the same inserted in them through auger holes. It should be a foot wide, with the sides three inches high. Animals can eat from both sides and nothing is wasted.

Of the miscellaneous stable tools I need say little, except to urge that each shall have a place and be kept there. A wooden broom back of the cow stalls is a good adjunct of the dung fork, and a common broom in the entry and aisles should be used daily.

Here is a handy wheelbarrow for the cow stables for moving bundles of straw and corn fodder. The construction of the front allows of good sized loads not possible in a common wheelbarrow.

The dairyman should know the capacity of his various measures, baskets and buckets in pounds, as well as in volume, since food rations are necessarily quoted in pounds. Milk pails can be made of a uniform weight; say two pounds exactly. It is then a simple and easy matter to accurately weigh the product of each cow as it is drawn, and at once record the weight.

The thermometer is a necessary thing in a stable, as without it there is danger of ill ventilation. The habit of looking at the temperature of the stable is a good one. Light and good ventilation are especially necessary in winter.

 A well-built dry goods box can easily be made into a very convenient feed chest by cutting it down in the manner shown. Let the lid project a little and cut out a place for the fingers in the front of the box. If the box is long enough, a partition can

be put in the middle for two kinds of grain.

It is a great convenience to have platform scales at the barn. Calves are to be weighed, rations made up, and things bought and sold. It tends toward accuracy.

It is important to save every pound of the urine. A feasible plan is to place horse manure daily in the gutter in rear of cows, and to sprinkle land plaster or kainit on this, or have the urine run from the gutter to a sunken hogshead; it should be saved by all means as it is the key to successful farming.

A little medicine chest or closet is almost a necessity, though its contents need not be very varied. It is well to have Epsom salts and a few other simple things within reach; also some bottles suitable for administering doses when occasion arises. The best dairying involves but little doctoring.

FIXINGS.

Make everything in the stable as plain and smooth as possible, avoiding corners and protruding timbers.

Don't try to economize overhead space—the more the room the better the air.

Two or three milk-fed cats at the barn are the best rat exterminators.

Keep things clean and bright.

Give personal attention to things.

A penny saved is a penny earned.

Cold draughts are the seeds of disease and loss.

A spring, or weight and pulley, on the cow stable door, is a good investment, as it insures against accidentally leaving it open.

The manure gutter should be hard enough and smooth enough to bear scrubbing with a splint broom. The feed trough should be of a shape to make washing easy; preferably low, flat and passing in front of all the cows. Walls and ceiling should be whitewashed.

AYRSHIRE COW.

Chapter XII.

THE GOOD MILKER.

Of all scrub stock the scrub milker is the worst.—Dorothy Tucker.

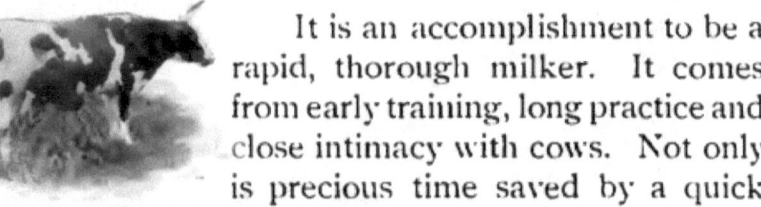

It is an accomplishment to be a rapid, thorough milker. It comes from early training, long practice and close intimacy with cows. Not only is precious time saved by a quick performance of the operation, but the cow's full capacity of production is encouraged. The precious liquid is drawn to the last drop, and the last drop is the richest of all.

The knack of milking is hard to describe; it comes by practice. The full teat is compressed by the hand in such a manner that the flow is downward, not back into the udder. A good milker will cause a perfect white shower to descend to the pail. In five minutes the udder is empty and the pail filled with froth-covered milk.

Good milking involves absolute cleanliness; a great many rapid milkers are unclean in their practices.

It is no uncommon thing, for instance, to milk wet; that is, the milker intentionally moistens his hands with milk, and then proceeds to fill the pail.

The practice does not really make milking easier, and it is too much like using the pail as a wash basin. It is altogether inexcusable.

To grasp the teats of a cow just after she has arisen from the bed in her stall, and to milk dry, is the other extreme. Dust, dirt and manure particles tumble freely into the pail.

The teats and udder should not be washed off, but

A FAVORITE.

wiped off with a dry cloth before milking. If water is used the teats will likely crack. A rough, loose cloth is best. Gunny-sack is splendid for this purpose. Then milk with hands dry.

It is strictly true that many so-called good dairies send out unclean milk; milk made unclean by the milkers. It is not only unclean, but is seeded with bacteria, which are the germs of decomposition.

I fear that a great many good milkers are guilty of carelessness. The proof is in the bottom of the milkman's serving can and in the bowl of the separator. The consumer too often finds black specks and worse in the bottom of the pitcher.

The good milker does not allow the full pail to remain in the stable, but carries it at once into another and cleaner atmosphere. He is not content with a coarse wire strainer, but uses a double thickness of good cheese cloth, which catches all the hairs and dust particles and other impurities which reach the pail under even the most careful management.

OLD WAY.

The newly drawn milk is at once cooled to say 50° F., either by placing the can in ice water and stirring with a paddle or by means of a

THE GOOD MILKER. 65

cooler. This favors the escape of the so-called "steam," and also of the "cow odor," and the milk is then ready for the delivery cans or bottles.

The cooling of the milk should be done only in a pure atmosphere ; not in the stable nor in a room opening into the stable.

There are various milk coolers on the market, and the choice of one should involve two considerations: efficiency and ease of cleaning after use. The method of running the milk over cold plates is preferable to that of running it through pipes, as the former device is more certain to be clean and free from taint.

The speedy removal of the animal heat from cows' milk is perhaps the most important requisite for good keeping quality.

MILK COOLER, NEW WAY.

It is bad policy to milk a cow while she is eating. After a while she will not be disposed to stand to be milked unless she has something to eat.

A great many kicking cows might be cured and more prevented, by simply trimming the finger nails often enough to keep them from cutting the teats.

Be quiet while milking. Pet the cows. Talk when you get through. They will soon learn to expect a caress and it pays.

The udder must be emptied to the last drop, and if this is not done every time the supply will fall short every time—that is, nature, finding that more milk has been produced than is required, will abstain from producing so much milk, and devote the food to the production of fat or of muscle.

The tidy milker should wear an apron like this. It can be made from a salt bag washed out and hemmed. It should have strong cords attached to it to tie around the body, and should be cut open in front for a little distance from the bottom to make it easier to hold the milk pail.

There are two things gained by warming the milk pail in winter; first, the milk froths and foams and does not splatter and splash all over the person milking, and second, the milk that is milked into a cold pail will not show the cream as thick or rich as when warm and foamy, and further, the quart or two of hot water carried to the barn to keep the pail warm can be put into a pail of water given the cow to drink, which is good for her.

A simple device, easily applied, to keep a cow from switching her tail, is a heavy rope or light trace chain, made in a loop, to throw over the rump. This will prevent a good deal of switching by both man and beast.

CO BOSS!

When you are angry don't kick the cow. Kick the milking stool till you break yourself of the kicking habit.

The milking stool is not a good hammer.

To be overharsh with a cow is like wasting a quart of milk.

Cows that leak their milk should be milked three times a day.

There is no self-milking device which is a success.

A slow milker will dry up a cow.

Some cows are born kickers, some become kickers, and many more have kicking abused into them.

Don't cool off the stables before milking. It makes the cows hold up their milk, and frequently they become fretful and kick.

Chapter XIII.

MILK AND CREAM.

Milk is not a miraculous dispensation.—John Tucker.

In 100 pounds of good milk there are about 87 pounds of water, 4 pounds of fat, 5 pounds of milk sugar, 3.3 pounds of casein and albumen, and .7 pound of mineral matter or salt, the latter consisting mainly of phosphates and chlorides. The proportions vary. The total solids (everything except the water) may be as high as 18 per cent. or as low as 10 per cent. The fat varies from 2 per cent. to 7 per cent., with 4 per cent. as an average. The cheese maker can get along with 3 per cent., but prefers 3.5 per cent.

Skimmilk Milk Cream Colostrum

FAT GLOBULES.

Milk laws in certain states and cities demand not less than 3 to 3.5 per cent. of fat and 9 to 9.5 per cent. of solids not fat. This means total solids of 12 or 13 per cent.

It is a great mistake to regard fat as the only valuable part of milk, though fat is a good index, because the more fat the larger the percentage of total solids.

A quart of milk weighs about 2.15 pounds, and a quart of cream about 2.10 pounds.

I am sorry to introduce so many figures and percentages, for they are not pleasant reading, but there is no help for it. The profits of dairying depend on details, and the details are legion.

The amount of fat in the milk of the same cow varies from time to time, from causes not always fully understood. The percentage differs greatly when some breeds are compared with others. The fat globules are actually larger in some breeds than others. Hence the cream rises more quickly and completely with the so-called butter cows.

Many dairymen who retail their milk to private consumers find it advantageous to have both large milkers and rich milkers in the herd, in order to get quantity, quality and color.

There are certain changes in the milk natural to the progress of the period of lactation. As the cow gets along there is an increased percentage of total solids. There is a greater viscosity or stickiness in the body (serum) of the milk, and the cream rises more slowly.

Cream always rises most completely and most promptly if set soon after coming from the cow. Long journeys and continued agitation are hostile to cream gathering.

CREAM-OMETER.

Bad flavors in milk and cream are due to one or more of several causes. They may arise from dirt, from the volatile oils of improper foods, from hostile bacteria, or from ill health of the cow.

The first and last causes are inexcusable and avoidable. The second cause (overfeeding of cabbage, turnips, mangels, ensilage, garlic) is under control of the dairyman, and may be remedied by a change of time of feeding or reduction of amount of food.

The third cause (bacteria) is closely associated

with the first. Hostile ferments caused by bacteria may be the result of dirt entering the milk or may come from storage in an unclean atmosphere.

It is the sugar in milk which undergoes the quickest and greatest change when souring occurs. Sweet butter, as everybody knows, may be churned from sour cream. There is milk sugar in cream as well as in milk.

The subject of bacteria is an important one to the dairyman. There are many ferments caused by bacteria which are not yet fully understood, but enough is known to emphasize the need of cleanliness in dairy work. Some bacteria are distinctly favorable, just as others are unfavorable to good results. The friendly bacteria are now employed in our butter making in much the same way that we employ yeast in our bread making. Each starts a desired ferment.

The so-called preservatives of milk, widely advertised, are better let alone. They are germicides or antiseptics or bacteria killers. They contain salicylic acid, saltpetre, boric acid, borax or formaldehyde. They are not direct poisons, but seem to have a hurtful effect on the human system, often producing diarrhœa. In one sense they are adulterants. The United States Dispensatory says the use of salicylic acid should be prohibited. Preservatives are properly forbidden by law in some states and cities.

LAC-
TOMETER.

Milk is not commonly adulterated, except with preservatives or with water.

If milk be properly aerated and cooled to 45° or 50° when drawn there should be no trouble in keeping it (at 50°) for 24 or 36 hours; but it should never be suffered to stand around in pitchers or open dishes in warm places. Neither should it be placed in closets or refrigerators with strong-flavored foods. It should be kept in a separate ice box. Old tin vessels are likely to impart a bad taste to milk. Wooden vessels are unsuitable, as they cannot be cleaned properly. Bright tin is good, while porcelain and glass are even better.

When it is necessary to keep milk a long time there are several ways of doing it. Pasteurization is one method; or the process may be carried up to the point of sterilization. Condensed milk is another form in which long-keeping quality is secured. These are all natural methods; which cannot be said of the results secured by preservatives.

Pasteurization is recommended for milk for babies, or when cold storage is not feasible. The requisite apparatus is simple, consisting essentially of a covered boiler. Bottles of milk are placed in the boiler (not on the bottom, but on supports or a false bottom), with cold water around them to a height above the height of the milk in the bottles. Stoppers of absorbent cotton are to be used; but not ordinary corks, as they are not to be trusted for cleanliness. The required temperature is 157° to 160° F. The heat is to be maintained for half an hour, when the bottles are to be cooled as quickly as possible and kept in a cool place, and left closed until used.

PASTEURIZING APPARATUS.

Sterilized milk is made at a higher temperature; almost or quite the boiling point. The albumen is likely to coagulate and form a scum.

The words "pasteurize" and "sterilize" are not

yet used in a strictly accurate sense. In popular language any method of destroying bacteria by a high temperature is "sterilizing," whereas to produce actual and complete sterilization necessitates the repeated heating of the milk to the boiling point for three successive days. This is to kill not only the bacteria, but the spores of the bacteria; the latter not being destroyed by a single boiling. Sterilization can be accomplished in a shorter time by heating to 248°, but this is possible only under pressure, as water boils at 212°. Pasteurization is usually sufficient, so far as health is concerned, if the milk is to be used soon. In both processes the sealing and quick cooling are essential parts of the operation.

There is no known simple test to determine the presence of disease germs in milk, and hence the necessity for the processes just described.

Condensed milk is made by sterilizing ordinary milk under pressure and evaporating say one-half its water, when it is put in tin or glass and hermetically sealed. It will thus keep indefinitely. There are two processes, one involving the addition of common sugar and one without sugar. The manufacture of condensed milk is becoming an American industry. It has long been carried on in Switzerland.

Milk when about to sour will coagulate when boiled. Farrington, of Wisconsin, has devised an alkaline tablet for determining the amount of acid, without boiling. The tablet solution with fresh milk produces a pink color. With milk about to sour this pink color is but faintly shown or is absent. This inexpensive test is suited to household use.

Ropy milk is probably the result of the presence of hostile bacteria, presumably in the pasture. It is extremely annoying to dairymen. A change of pasture is the only remedy that I can recommend with confidence.

DRIPPINGS.

Freshness in milk is as much a matter of care as a matter of hours.

Freshly drawn milk is sterile. The dairyman decides what species of bacteria shall enter it.

Cool the milk quickly. It is the secret of good keeping qualities.

The cream from some cows is so slow in rising that it does not rise until after skimming and not then.

Night's milk is richer than morning's.

It is said that milk does not quench thirst like water. It is more victuals than drink.

Cream is 15 per cent. lighter than the milk. This is why it rises to the surface.

Condensed milk, in proportion to uncondensed, is one to four. The water is driven out and the solids retained. By adding water it is milk again, though not exactly as it comes from the cow.

Boiling milk makes it more easily digested. It will also kill the germs which may cause purging.

Leaving the milk in the stable till it gets cold makes less cream.

The milk of cows in calf will get thick and ropy sooner if fed all dry and heating foods.

I do not know anything which will take garlic out of milk better than pigs in the pasture.

Who hath woe? Who hath redness of eyes? Verily, it is she that crieth over spilt milk.—*Source unknown.*

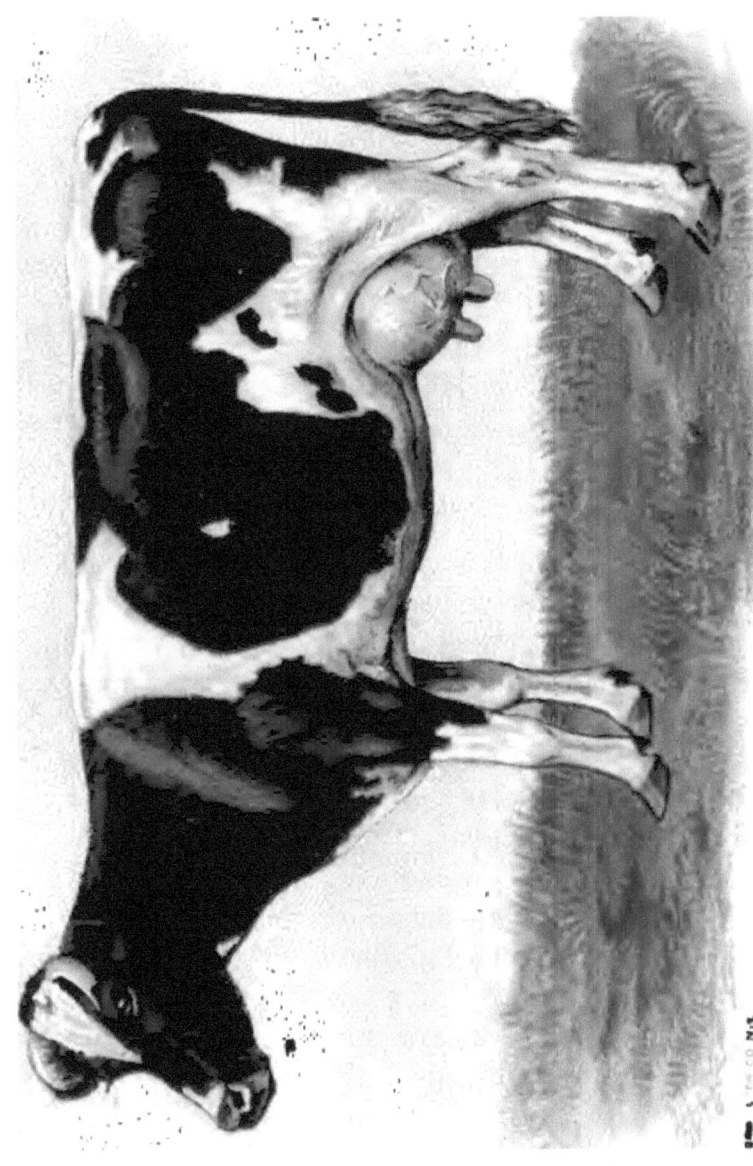

HOLSTEIN-FRESIAN COW.

Chapter XIV.

BUTTER.

Not merely gilt-edge, but solid gold all through; the only genuine gold bricks in the world.—Tim.

Cream is an article which varies considerably in its composition. Snyder's "Chemistry of Dairying" quotes the following average analysis of twenty-five samples:

```
                              Per cent.
Water . . . . . . . . . . . . . . . 66.41
Fat      . . . . . . . . . . . . . . 25.72
Casein and albumen . . . . . . . . 3.70
Milk sugar . . . . . . . . . . . . . 3.54
Ash . . . . . . . . . . . . . . . . .63
```

It will be seen that the total solids amount to 33.59 per cent.; that is, cream is about two-thirds water and one-third solids. According to Snyder the fat in cream varies all the way from 10 to 60 per cent., with an average of 20 or 25 per cent.

The total solids of milk, it will be remembered, amount to about 12 or 13 per cent. Cream has the same ingredients as milk, but in different proportions; that is, none of the milk ingredients are wholly absent from cream.

Butter is usually regarded as consisting of fat and fat only, but the chemist finds in it all the milk and cream ingredients, possibly excepting albumen. The following

CHURNING WHEN HARRIET WAS A GIRL.

figures represent the average of twenty analyses of butter made by the Minnesota Experiment Station:

	Per cent.
Water	12.00
Fat	85.00
Ash and salt	2.25
Casein and milk sugar	.75

Butter should not contain less than 83 per cent. of fat, though the amount varies; nor more than 15 per cent. of water.

An examination of the analysis of butter will show at a glance why it is customary to add, say, one-sixth of the known weight of butter fat in a given quantity of milk in estimating in advance the product of butter.

One-sixth is 16.6 per cent. To allow for inevitable losses it is considered safer in making estimates of butter to add only 15 per cent. of the actual weight of fat in the milk.

The main object in cream gathering is the manufacture of butter, although large quantities of cream are now sold for domestic use. The ice cream makers also use considerable amounts. When a good cream trade can be secured, the best cash results are to be had in that way, as cream is more of an article of luxury than butter.

There are two systems of cream gathering practised in America, one depending on gravity and the other on centrifugal force.

The gravity plan offers a choice between shallow and deep setting. In shallow setting use is made of tin pans or glazed earthen crocks. The depth of milk is two to six inches. A great surface is exposed to the air, and there is constant danger of contamination from dust particles. This plan is often practised in private families, the milk being set in closets, pantry shelves, cellars or spring houses. It usually sours quickly. The plan is not the best, though good products are obtainable under strict cleanliness.

The deep-setting method, which is next in efficiency to the separator, makes use of round cans made of heavy tin, about 8 inches in diameter and 18 to 26 inches in depth. These cans set in ice water produce very satisfactory results in from 12 to 24 hours. The cream may be removed from the surface, or the skimmilk may be drawn off from beneath by a small spigot at the bottom of the can. The loss of fat may be reduced by the deep setting system (according to Plumb) to .17 of one per cent., as against a loss of .34 of one per cent. in surface skimming. Cheap tin vessels should never be used, as the milk and cream are tainted as soon as the tin has worn off the iron.

CREAM SETTING CAN.

In 100 pounds of 4 per cent. milk the lost fat in shallow setting would amount to .34 of a pound, or 8½ per cent. of the total fat, while the lost fat in deep setting would amount to only .17 of a pound, or 4¼ per cent. of the total fat. The deep system is therefore better.

Deep setting in spring water is good, but a cabinet creamer is better, on account of the use of ice. These devices are, however, being largely replaced by mechanical separators.

CABINET CREAMER.

"Sweet cream butter" is not in

general demand in America. It has been put upon the market from time to time, and is now manufactured in certain localities, but is usually bought only for special purposes. The sweet product made by the Swedish butter extractor, in 1889 and later, found but few patrons, and the extractor itself appears to have practically disappeared from the American market. As reported upon by the Delaware station it obtained only 84.60 pounds of butter out of a possible 100, as against 93.94 pounds obtained by a cream separator and churn.

Sour cream butter is in general favor in the United States. The sourness is caused by lactic acid, and the lactic acid is caused by or accompanied by well-known bacteria of several species.

Cream, whether obtained by gravity or by separator, must be "ripened" in order to secure the desired butter flavor. Long experience and best methods have established a standard of excellence in butter; and the butter maker must needs cater to this popular taste.

Among recent important discoveries in the science of dairying is the fact that the ferments of milk and cream are under human control; that bacteria cultures may be prepared on a commercial scale for use in butter making just as yeast is used in bread making; and that these ferment starters tend to make an exact science of what formerly was guesswork.

The widely-advertised bacteria cultures for producing a certain much-desired butter flavor are nothing more nor less than preparations which start the ferments which come naturally in all good dairies under most favorable circum-

DAIRY THERMOMETER.

stances. Butter made under the best conditions of breed, feed, care and treatment, without artificial aid, is the pattern which the bacteria culturist successfully imitates. The cultures merely start the souring in the right direction.

The process of ripening cream is hastened by stirring and aerating. The time required is about twenty-four hours. No new or sweet cream should be added at churning time, or within twelve hours previously, as it will be mostly lost; or else the ripened cream will be overchurned.

The temperature for churning sour cream, well ripened, should be about 60° F. in summer and 65° F. in winter. For churning sweet cream the proper temperature is 50° to 55°.

A small amount of butter color is allowable, without conflicting with the food laws against adulteration. Annatto (Bixa orellana) or some other vegetable preparation should be used, but not aniline dye. The use of carrots in the cow manger is to be recommended.

OLD FASH-IONED CHURN.

Churning should be a quick, cleanly operation. The washing and working involve details of individual choice and experience. Salting is a matter of market. Three-quarters of an ounce of salt to the pound is a good average quantity. The salt should not show a tendency to absorb water or to become hard and lumpy. There are better brands on the market.

Printing and packing demand precision of method. It always pays to make a neat print for the retail market, and to put the lump in fresh butter paper. A nickel's worth of care will add a dime to the market value.

White oak vessels (tubs, kegs, firkins) are suitable for butter-packing purposes. They must be perfectly clean, and should be soaked in brine before being used. The butter is packed in a two-inch layer; then sprinkled with salt; then a two-inch layer of butter, etc. The top is covered with a white muslin cloth.

Pasteurized butter is butter made from pasteurized cream. It is deemed unwise to expect success with any special bacteria as a starter without first using heat to destroy the ferments already present in the cream, which may be of an undesirable kind.

In closing I will briefly summarize the whole process of butter making for the benefit of the novice.

First, put clean, sweet cream into a jar or can in a cool, well-ventilated place, where there are no suspicious odors. Bad odors will make bad butter. Stir the cream gently at least twice a day. The cellar or milk room temperature should be from 55° to 65°. At this temperature the cream will sour or ripen inside of forty-eight hours with a characteristic fragrance which cannot be mistaken when once learned. No fresh cream should be added to the jar within twelve hours of churning, as it will not ripen and will be mostly lost. Sweet cream can be churned, but its churning time and temperature are different from sour cream. Churning should be done frequently for best results—twice a week at least.

On churning days scald the churn and then rinse it with cold water. Use a dairy thermometer in the cream, and make the temperature 65° in winter or 60° in summer. Add a little butter color, if desired, as per directions on the bottle. Churn steadily—neither fast nor slow. The butter will come, under ordinary circumstances, in half an hour.

Churn slowly at the last until the butter becomes granulated the size of kernels of wheat. Draw the buttermilk and wash in two waters; cold, clear water. Salt in the churn and mix the salt in well. After salting let it stand fifteen minutes for the salt to dissolve. Then work in the churn, either by churning or with paddles, until it becomes one mass. Then it is ready to ball or put into tub or box.

Never employ a man in the dairy who uses tobacco. The fumes of tobacco smoke are exceedingly penetrating and lasting, and will surely affect the butter.

No butter, however well made, will retain all its flavor and aroma more than ten days or two weeks.

Working butter too much, or when too cold, breaks the grain and gives it a salvy appearance that lessens its market value. Such butter soon loses flavor and becomes rancid.

BUTTER WORKER.

"If you want your butter both nice and sweet
    Don't turn with nervous jerking,
  But ply the dasher slowly, and then
    You'll hardly know that you're working;
  And when the butter has come, you'll say
    'Yes, surely, this is the better way—'
                  Churn Slowly."

A damp or hot place will not do to store butter. The store-room must be dry, sweet and cool. Cover with damp salt and a cloth.

GRANULES.

Cheap parchment paper sometimes moulds and causes mouldy butter.

We should be sending more butter abroad.

It is better to keep ten 300-pound cows than twenty 150-pound cows. Six times the profit in the former.

Butter making is an art suited to women.

Bad butter is oleo's best friend.

It costs as much to make butter that will sell for soap grease, as a first-class article that will sell at a fancy price.

Conceit will not make good butter.

Butter loses by storage.

Don't hurry the cows to or from the pasture. If you do you will have to hurry the butter to market or lose your trade.

Better churn twice than mix cream in different stages of ripening.

Look forward to a winter dairy.

There is a big difference between the cash and trading out the butter.

The average farm-house cellar is an unnatural butter kingdom.

A good butter maker is a sun worshipper and a hot water crank.

Chapter XV.

IMITATIONS.

There is fraud somewhere when an article must be misnamed in order to sell it.—John Tucker.

The adulteration of foods is widely practised, and dairy products form no exception to the general rule. Fortunately the law is taking note of such frauds, and food commissioners are at work to protect the public against deception.

Bogus butter is mainly of two kinds, known respectively as oleomargarine and butterine.

These products are made of beef fat, and are in one sense by-products of beef slaughtering operations in the great cities. Fats of various grades of cleanness and uncleanness are put through filter presses, and the fats thus graded. The harder fats are used for the manufacture of soap and candles.

The softer fats are put into churns with sweet milk, and then churned, colored, salted, and packed to resemble butter in both taste and appearance. The products are sold as oleomargarine and butterine.

There is a slight difference between the melting points of these two articles. Butterine is sold in the northern markets, frequently in illegal competition with genuine butter. Oleomargarine is sent South and is also largely exported.

Cheese is adulterated by a substitution of lard and cottolene oil for the real butter fat of milk, the milk

To prepare an infusion the stomach, or a portion of it, is steeped in warm water or whey, and bottled.

To have good rennet, of known strength, is of prime importance in cheese making.

The working and manipulation of the curd demands experience. Flavor is determined largely at this stage of the process. Some cheese makers employ spices and aromatic herbs and even liquors, in the production of certain brands of cheese.

An accurate thermometer should be employed in cheese-making operations. Though there are many ways of making good cheese, each way demands accuracy of detail.

Cheese is made of whole milk, of whole milk with cream added, of partly skimmed milk, of skimmed milk, of cream; and even buttermilk is employed in making some so-called cheeses.

Filled cheese, sometimes called oleo cheese or lard cheese, is made by combining oleo oil with skimmed milk.

Full cream cheese, honestly made, is of course the best; though some of the fancy cheeses, made with special care, command higher prices.

Skill in manipulating the curd in its early stages must be supplemented by equal skill in the curing of the cheese. The ripening process is of great importance.

The factory process of cheese making in America may be briefly outlined as follows: The milk is received twice a day. The evening milk is kept over night at 60°, and then thoroughly mixed with morning's milk and heated to 80°. Rennet is added in sufficient quantity to bring the curd in an hour. When the curd has become sufficiently solid to split before the finger it is cut with implements called curd knives into small cubes. The vat is then heated gradually to 95° or 96°, and the heat is maintained for an hour or more. Difference in time makes a difference in the ultimate hardness or firmness of the cheese.

At the conclusion of the heating or cooking the curd is well-stirred, to facilitate the separation of the whey. After a slight acidity has developed the whey is drawn off, and the curd allowed to cool.

It is next torn to fragments, and when sufficiently firm is ground into small pieces and salted at the rate of two pounds per 100 of curd or 1000 pounds of milk used. The curd is then ready for pressing and curing.

The curing-room, a necessary feature of a cheese-making establishment, is an apartment provided with capacious shelving. The temperature and moisture should be uniform and the ventilation good. The cheeses, properly bandaged, require frequent turning and considerable time for their proper ripening. The American standard cheese weighs sixty pounds.

For producing small cheeses at home, away from a factory, make curd by the use of rennet, as already described. A new wash-tub or other large receptacle may be employed as a vat. A cheese hoop may be made from a cheese-box from the grocery store. A head or follower can be sawed out to fit the hoop, and a lever press made with a flat fence-rail. Or a number of small moulds can be made of tin fruit cans, with tops and bottoms unsoldered.

Mix well-stirred night's milk with morning's milk, as already described, and heat to 88°. Use a teaspoonful of coloring to 150 pounds of milk, and enough rennet to curdle in fifteen minutes.

After cutting the curd raise to a temperature of 102°. This can be done by dipping off the whey, heating it, and returning it to the curd, all the while stirring gently.

When the curd particles seem elastic, and fall apart when gently pressed with the hand, the whey may be removed, except enough to cover the curd.

The curd is placed in the moulds, and light pressure applied. In half an hour the cheeses should be ready for bandaging with muslin—a strip around the circumference and a piece for top and another for bottom. The cloths should be dipped into hot water (120°) before application.

The cheeses thus wrapped, and further protected by pieces of muslin, are returned to the moulds, tops downward, and gradually subjected to heavy pressure, which should continue for a day.

To ripen the cheeses they should be kept in an airy cellar, and turned daily for five or six days, each time rubbing them with salt. The temperature of the cellar should be 65° to 70°. After the salting has ceased the cheeses should be turned and rubbed with the hand daily, and then two or three times a week. In two or three weeks they will be ready for use. If they become mouldy they should be washed in strong brine.

STILTON CHEESE. The most famous of the double cream cheeses, the Stilton, is produced almost exclusively in Leicestershire, England, where the milk from cows grazing on sweet, rich pasture without artificial food is considered best. It is made from the morning's milk to which cream from the previous night's mess has been added in the proportion of one part cream to ten or twelve of milk. The curd is shaped in the hoop without pressure. To develop the blue mold that is an essential feature of this brand the curing is done in a warm room and sometimes bits of old cheese are put in the new.

Pot Cheese. For the most delicious pot cheese the following recipe from a successful New York maker can be depended upon: To ten quarts of buttermilk add three quarts of skimmilk. Heat it slowly, and when the curd has risen dip it off carefully and put it in a thin cloth to drain. Add butter to suit the degree of richness required, and salt to the taste, mixing all thoroughly.

Edam. This cheese gets its name from a town in Holland. It is the nearly globular, reddish-colored cheese now widely sold in all leading American grocery stores.

Sage. Sage cheese may be made in a small dairy. This is one of the so-called green cheeses. Green sage, parsley and marigold leaves are used in the process of manufacture.

Neufchatel. An American brand of this French cheese is to be had in our large cities. The cheese is a pasty substance, to be spread on bread after the fashion of butter.

Brie. This is a French cheese which is now made in America. It is of a soft, almost creamy, consistency.

ROQUEFORT. This is another cheese depending for its flavor largely upon fungous growths.

CHEDDAR. English Cheddar is regarded as the best plain cheese in the world, and American Cheddar is quite similar to it. The whole milk is warmed to 80°, and the curd broken into fine pieces. Curd and whey are brought to 100°, and the whey drawn off when a certain degree of acidity has been reached. It is salted at the rate of two pounds to 100 pounds of curd.

PINEAPPLE. This is one of the small, high-priced cheeses in favor in America. It pays to make such goods.

SKIPPERS.

In round figures it requires ten pounds of milk to make a pound of cheese and twenty pounds of milk to make a pound of butter.

Cow's milk is not fit for cheese until the calf is a week old.

Can you not invent a nice little cheese for a nice little retail trade of your own?

It is cheese, not butter, that carries fertility from the farm; $12.30 to the ton of whole-milk cheese.

A ton of skimmilk cheese is credited with fertilizing value to the amount of $23.55.

A slow coming and curing cheese is best.

Cured whole-milk cheese contains about one-third fat and a little less than one-third casein and albumen and one-third water.

Every shade of cowy or animal odor and taint can be eliminated from cheese by airing the warm curd, provided *sweet rennet* is used and the curd is gotten out of the whey and the airing is done before acidity sets in.

The digestibility of cheese depends mainly on the presence of the phosphates of lime, iron, soda and magnesia. These are dissolved by acid and washed out in the whey. By drawing off the whey when sweet, or just on the verge of acidity, they are nearly all retained and the cheese is digestible.

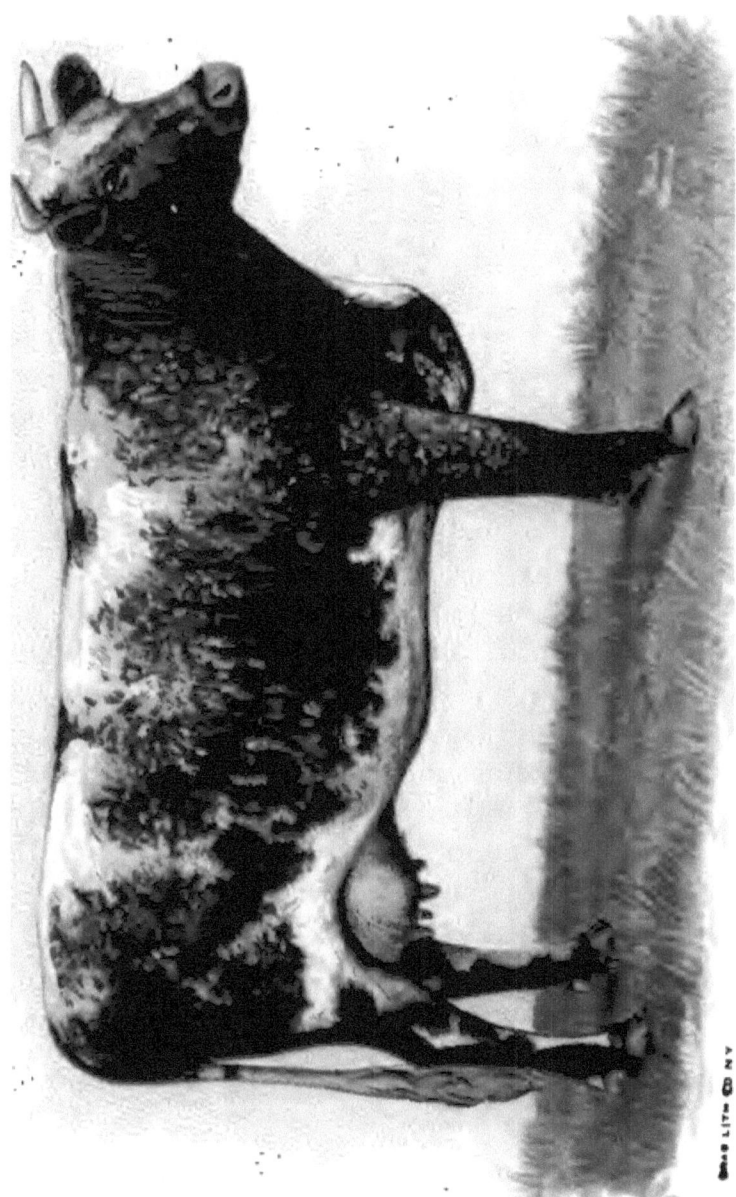

Chapter XVII.

BEEF.

Some folks want a steer and a cow all in one animal—beef and butter. It is a partnership which does not work well. —John Tucker.

The commercial profits of beef production depend largely on location and conditions. Beefing in a dairying district does not pay, nor does dairying in a beef district. Close to the large eastern cities the dairy cow is at her best, and feeding steers is at a discount. In the West, where not adjacent to good local dairying markets, the fattening of steers for shipment is a profitable industry.

There are also intermediate districts where milk and beef are both in demand, and where heavy cows are able to supply both.

Even in the East some dairymen make a habit of buying large-framed cows when fresh, feeding them heavily, milking them as long as profitable, and then selling them to the butcher, replacing them with other animals with calves by their sides. To supply this demand is the business of some drovers, who buy the fresh cows in districts remote from the large cities and ship them in carload lots and sell them at public auction.

The heavy breeds of cattle are adapted to the needs of the cheese maker rather than the butter maker.

The smaller breeds are not in high favor with the butchers, who complain that the meat is yellow and less salable than where the fat is white in color. Fancy and prejudice go a long way, even in beefsteaks. It is therefore better, in buying cows to fatten, to select those of square build, rather than small, triangle-shaped animals. The butcher always looks at the hip bones and at the rump. The choice cuts and best prices pertain to that end of the animal.

The business of beef production involves a careful study of economic principles. Carefully conducted experiments show that steers like cows must be fed on a well balanced ration; that such a ration produces more gain and more profit than a poorly balanced ration; that such beef actually has a higher market value per pound than the beef from animals fed on a poorly constructed ration; and that the ordinary corn and cob meal used by farmers is unprofitable, when used alone, as it requires the addition of some highly nitrogenous food like wheat bran or cottonseed meal to make it fully advantageous.

Sometimes it is feasible, even in the East, to buy steers in the autumn for winter feeding on terms that admit of financial profit. Whenever this plan will fully pay the cash outlay, and leave a big manure pile as clear profit, it is to be commended. The manure of a steer well fed for six months should be worth from $10 to $15.

In raising calves for steers the early feeding should be right. Castration should occur at the age of six months, and the animal should be fit for the butcher when two years old. It is believed that profits lie mainly in early maturity wherever high feeding is practised.

In making a fattening or beef-producing ration for a dairy cow we have no better ingredient than corn meal. It is practically the same with the steer. In all cases the ration must be balanced, or the excess of corn meal will simply go to the dung heap.

Here are two suggested rations for steers weighing 1000 pounds, the ration in each case to cover a whole day:

10 lbs. shelled corn.
5 lbs. wheat bran.
4 lbs. linseed meal (new process).
10 lbs. corn fodder (dry).
3 lbs. wheat straw.
40 lbs. corn ensilage.
5 lbs. clover hay.
10 lbs. finely ground corn meal.
3 lbs. cottonseed meal.

A "BEEFY" COW AND CALF.

The latter is, I think, distinctly better in calling for finely ground corn meal instead of whole corn. The cottonseed meal should be divided so as not to all come in either of the three daily meals. It is a highly concentrated food.

Corn silage is of great value in a ration for fattening steers, but a ration of silage and corn meal alone is not safe. A mixture of straw or chaff with the silage and meal renders it safe—one pound of straw to every three pounds of silage.

The daily gain in weight grows less as cattle grow older. Steers matured and marketed at two years old give thirty per cent. more profit than if kept till three.

A 1000-pound steer requires an average of eleven pounds of feed to make one pound of gain.

A juicy, tender young beef should be one of the good things a grazing farm produces for family use every fall. November and December are good months for slaughtering, as the meat can be kept fresh nearly all winter.

Neighborhood beef clubs are in favor in some places. These clubs are conducted on various plans. The idea is co-operative, and the details are arranged to suit the members. A score of families, more or less, join together and agree that a beef shall be killed and divided every week. This would mean twenty pounds of fresh meat to each family from a beef dressing 400 pounds. Each member in turn furnishes the animal. It is found best to have the slaughtering always done in the same place.

GOOD ONES.

DRIED BEEF.

A cold animal may shiver off many pounds of flesh. Give the fattening steer a teaspoonful of salt daily. Beef the rogue cows.

Veal the male calves or beef them. Don't monkey them.

To grow animals, feed one thing; to fatten them another.

Don't get the steers to kicking. They can be coaxed better than whipped out of it.

The most profit in the steer is in the first year's growth. The next year has less, and so on.

Don't try to make the corn in the steer's belly take the place of shelter.

Chapter XVIII.

BY-PRODUCTS.

"Gather up the fragments that nothing be lost."

Milk, cream, butter and cheese are the main products of the dairy. The minor or by-products include skimmilk, cottage cheese or smearcase, whey and buttermilk. Calves are in one sense a by-product, but need no mention in this chapter. Manure is a by-product of great importance.

For purposes of comparison it is well to have the (average) ingredients of milk and its by-products arranged compactly expressed in percentages, as follows:

	Water.	Fat.	Casein and Albumen (Protein.)	Sugar.	Ash.
Whole Milk	87.50	3.50	3.25	5.00	.75
Skimmilk	90.25	.20	3.60	5.15	.80
Buttermilk	90.50	.20	3.30	5.30	.70
Whey	93.00	.35	.80	5.20	.65

[The percentage of fat varies greatly; 3.50 per cent. is too low for butter profits.]

To emphasize the value of the by-products of milk as fertilizers the following will be found useful:

	Nitrogen.	Phosphoric Acid.	Potash.
Whole Milk	.53	.19	.18
Skimmilk	.56	.20	.19
Buttermilk	.48	.17	.16
Whey	.15	.14	.18

This indicates that a ton of whole milk is worth as a

fertilizer about $2.04, a ton of skimmilk about $2.15, a ton of buttermilk about $1.84, and a ton of whey about 83 cents. When these farm products are sold they carry away with them fertility to the amount stated. The milk of a cow for a year (5000 pounds or 2½ tons) would therefore carry away about $5.00 in the shape of fertilizers. If the cow's annual manure product is worth $19.00 this $5.00 must be deducted, leaving a net gain of only $14.00 for the manure.

These figures show the wisdom of feeding the by-products of milk on the farm, unless they can be sold. Of course where they can be well marketed it is good business policy to do so, afterward investing part of the proceeds in artificial manures.

I have been compelled to refer frequently to the term balanced ration, and whole milk may be used as an example. This article is an almost perfect food, especially adapted to the body-growth of young animals.

As milk is nearly all digestible the above analysis may be used as it stands. The rule says: Multiply the digestible fat by 2¼ and add to the digestible carbohydrates. This gives the sum total of the non-nitrogenous elements, the fat being multiplied by 2¼ on account of its superior value as a heat producer. Then divide by the digestible protein and the result will indicate the nutritive ratio. That is, if the quotient be 4 the ratio is said to be as 1 to 4, as in the case of whole milk. Hence we say that a ratio of 1 to 4 is the proper one for young, growing animals.

It seems almost contradictory to say that, bulk for bulk, skimmilk is richer than new milk in protein (casein and albumen), but such is the case. Dairymen should remember this in preparing the calf ration. It is not because anything has been added, but because the renewal of one element (the fat) increases the percentage (not the quantity) of the remaining elements.

Skimmilk is an excellent and nutritious food for man or beast, but whether used in the kitchen or in the dairy it should be supplemented by foods containing sugars and starches (carbonaceous foods) for reasons already explained. It is quite as important that human rations should be as well-balanced as stock rations.

The sale of skimmilk should be encouraged by law, not discouraged. It is a wholesome food, and a perfectly honest article when sold under its true name.

As a food for calves, pigs or even cows it is excellent. It may be fed sweet or sour; preferably the former. Milk soured in a proper, cleanly manner is not unwholesome, but when permitted to sour in a filthy barrel it is liable to produce bowel troubles in young stock. Calves are sure to get the scours. Pigs appear to have stomachs made of cast-iron, but it is different with calves; and I am sure it would be profitable to practise cleanliness even with pigs.

Cottage cheese or smearcase is an article of general home consumption and market sale in Pennsylvania and other states. It is simply sour milk with the whey drained off. The residue, which is mainly casein, is in reality a cheese. It is salted and made into balls for sale, or is sold by the dipperful. On the table it is often prepared by adding cream, salt, pepper, etc., to increase its palatability. It is a cheap, wholesome, nutritious food, especially if eaten with fruit, either raw or cooked.

Whey consists mostly of water and sugar, as shown in the analysis. It is valuable for food, especially for pigs. To balance up a ration including whey the use of wheat bran would be advisable; not corn meal, as the latter would be too much like adding carbohydrates to carbohydrates.

WE CALL THIS ONE "BUTTERMILK."

Buttermilk is somewhat like skimmilk in composition, as will be seen by the analysis. It has some value as a beverage, and is sold for that purpose; but its usual destination is the swill-tub. It is a useful food for the reasons that were mentioned in the case of skimmilk. Corn meal should be used with it rather than bran, as it is already rich in protein.

Now that the buffalo has become nearly extinct we must look to cattle to supply us with carriage robes, and they will do it. I am now the possessor of a splendid robe made from a Galloway steer, and much prefer it to my buffalo robe. It is not so heavy, it is more flexible, and almost as warm. Preferably such robes are made from hides taken from animals in cold climates, that have wintered outdoors. Such robes can be bought at a moderate price, or a farmer can send a hide to the tanners and have it returned made into a robe.

It is estimated that the loss to butchers, farmers and trappers in this country from wrong methods of removing and curing hides exceeds one million dollars annually. Figure 1 shows the right way of removing beef and calf hides and shows the shape of the hides when so removed. On the fore leg the cut should be made down to the armpit, then forward to the point of brisket as shown by dotted lines. On the hind leg the knife should also follow the dotted lines. Figure 2 shows how not to do it and the result of the wrong method. Never cut across the throat. Always take out the horns and tailbone and fill the cavity from which the bone is removed with salt or alum water. To salt a sixty pound hide requires a water-bucket of salt. Rub on well and roll up. By keeping back of knife close to hide and drawing firmly with the left, cutting or scoring will be prevented.

FIG. 1.

Lastly I must say a word about manure, a by-product of the dairy of the greatest economic importance; a thing too often treated carelessly, with consequent financial loss.

The manure from well-fed cows is estimated to be worth $2.00 per ton, and the yearly product, if it were possible to save all, nearly ten tons, or a total of not less than $19.00. Of all the foods given to the cow some eighty per cent. (in fertility) goes to the dung pile.

FIG. 2.

The best known preservatives of manure in storage are such things as gypsum, kainit, etc. They absorb the ammonia that would otherwise be lost. A German authority recommends for daily use the following per 880-pounds weight of cow: Superphosphate, 1 pound, 2 ounces; gypsum, 1 pound, 12 ounces; kainit, 1 pound, 5 ounces. The European people take good care of stable manure.

I wish to call attention to the statements of chemists as to the relative value of solid and liquid cow manure. Take the item of nitrogen, for instance, which is by far the most expensive and valuable part of natural and artificial manures. A ton of fresh cattle excrement contains: Nitrogen, 5.8 pounds; potash, 2 pounds; phosphoric acid, 3.4 pounds. A ton of urine contains: Nitrogen, 11.6 pounds; potash, 9.8 pounds. Computing nitrogen at 15 cents, potash at 5½ cents and phosphoric acid at 8 cents per pound, the respective values are $1.25 for the ton of excrement, and $2.28 for the urine.

GALLOWAY BULL AND COW.

Chapter XIX.

WINTER.

December is as pleasant as May to the well-kept cow.—Tim.

Winter dairying is no more difficult and is in many respects more satisfactory than summer dairying. It costs no more to feed the cows, and it is easier to properly care for the milk. In winter the flies are absent, and the ferments which make trouble are less active. It is less of a problem to keep things warm in winter than to keep things cool in summer.

Of course it is cheaper to pasture cows than to feed them in the stall, but when all expenses are footed up, month by month, I find that there is not much difference among the twelve months of the year. Part of the summer wages are chargeable to winter, on account of the gathering of harvests and filling of silos, so the outlay is not wholly a matter of season.

A well-built cow stable is never cold. Hay, fodder, ensilage, feed, water should all be within convenient reach.

Preparation for winter dairying should begin the previous spring, with the planting of ensilage corn. This corn should have the best of culture, and should be treated just as field corn is treated until September. It has by that time fully matured, with well-glazed grains. It is then harvested, taken at once to the barn, run through a cutter, and put into the silo. Four tons per cow per year is a safe allowance. A cubic foot of packed silage weighs 40 pounds as previously stated.

Successional plantings of corn should be made for summer use in the dairy, to be fed on the soiling plan; that is, cut green and carried to the cows.

Provision should be made in advance so that all the cows shall drop their calves in the autumn, from October to November.

The food ration should have careful study, because with a stable of fresh cows it is desirable to work for best results in milk with least cost of material for food.

I fear that many dairymen burn up too much food for fuel; not literally, as some farmers burn corn, but in the stomachs of animals, for heating purposes. The barn is, perhaps, so cold that the animals must be converted into stoves.

"SNOW BALL."

The winter food of a cow must be both good and inexpensive. One of the most famous dairies within my knowledge a few years ago used the following winter ration daily: Eight pounds cut clover hay, 8 pounds wheat bran, 8 pounds corn meal, steamed and mixed. Of course a high-grade of milk was produced, and this dairy could afford the cost as its reputation was of the dollar-a-pound butter sort. This ration is too expensive for general use.

Ensilage is the main reliance now for winter feeding, and even the smaller dairies can afford a silo. A round silo can be constructed quite cheaply. The United States Department of Agriculture describes a round silo of 180 tons capacity, 20 feet inside diameter and 30 feet deep, which can be constructed at an estimated cost of $246.59. This is a cost of only $1.37 per ton of storage capacity.

Here are a few protein analyses of silage for comparison. They should set dairymen to thinking about the feeding possibilities of some other things beside corn silage:

	Average per cent. of protein.
Corn silage	1.7
Sorghum silage	0.8
Red clover silage	4.2
Soja bean silage	4.1
Cowpea silage	2.7
Field pea silage	5.9

Corn and sorghum are both grasses in fact. They are low in protein (nitrogen) the most expensive element of mill feeds. Clovers, beans and peas are all legumes, and are all rich in protein, and will quite certainly be used some day for silage purposes.

Taking corn silage (now in common use) as a basis for a good and cheap food for dairy cows, we begin with its analysis; or rather, with its digestible analysis, as follows:

	Protein.	Carbohydrates and Fat.	Nutritive ratio.
Corn silage	1.1	18.2	1 : 16.5

This food as it stands has a proportion of sugars and starches far in excess of the protein, and out of proper proportion. Instead of 1 : 16.5 we must try to get down to the Wisconsin ration (1 : 6.9) or preferably lower. The best and cheapest ingredients at hand are, say, clover hay and wheat bran. Hence I suggest the following, the cottonseed meal being introduced for balancing the ration; the ration to be divided so as to cover a day:

40 pounds corn silage,	5 pounds wheat bran,
8 " clover hay,	2 " cottonseed meal.

This ration is a good one, and is not expensive. Its nutritive ratio is about 1:5.9. Farmers must figure out the ratio best suited to themselves and their crops. A little figuring will enable a dairyman to substitute dry corn fodder for the ensilage in this ration if desired. In the latter case I would recommend the use of some roots or pumpkins.

SHIVERS.

A stanchion-held cow lying down is sometimes tramped on by a neighbor. Injured teats may result.

Winter dairying will never be overdone. Cold weather uses up the fat.

Every shiver of the cow shakes money out of the owner's pocket.

Do not, as soon as the first warm spring day comes, turn the cows out of their comfortable stable, and allow them to fill themselves with frost-bitten grass. It will only fill them, not feed them; then, too, it is a very unhealthy filling.

If winter feed is bought let it be in late summer; it is cheaper then.

Stone basement barns are apt to be dark, damp and chilly.

NO SHIVERS HERE.

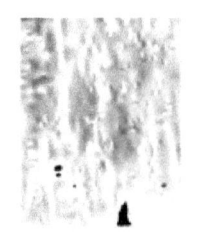

Chapter XX.

POINTS ON MARKETS.

Small profits and prompt settlements in cash.—John **Tucker's Plan.**

Happy is the dairyman who can join hands with the consumer, and thus save the middleman's sometimes too generous profits. This is not always possible, of course, because a great deal of milk, butter and cheese must be sold wholesale.

Speaking in general terms the cost of selling a perishable food product is just about equal to the cost of its production; that is, if it costs two cents a quart to produce milk it will cost somewhere near two cents a quart to retail it. Milk costing two cents should sell for at least three cents wholesale, and six cents retail. This would allow a margin of profit to both producer and retailer. These figures are used merely for illustration.

The margin of profit on butter is estimated on a different basis, because butter is far less perishable than milk, and the risk of carrying it in stock is less. It costs less to retail butter than milk because the holder of milk must sell it quickly, while the holder of butter is more independent and can wait a little for customers. The retail profits on butter usually are but a few cents a pound; perhaps just about as much per pound as the best producers make on each pound of their output.

The only certainty of dairy profits lies in leading instead of following the market; and every dairyman is really his own judge, fixing to a certainty the market price of his own product.

The old-fashioned forty-quart tin milk can is still in favor in Pennsylvania for shipping milk. In New England and elsewhere a much smaller can is used for shipping purposes.

In the Philadelphia retail trade the time-honored cans and serving kettles of a past generation are still to be seen, but their days are numbered.

The glass jar or bottle, with its close-fitting pasteboard cover (the cover to be used but once), is so evidently superior in every way to the old-fashioned tin utensil that glass is fast taking possession of the market.

Aside from cleanliness and fairness in distribution of cream, the glass jar is superior in accuracy of measurement.

One of the agricultural papers lately published a letter from a farmer bearing directly on this point. A retail milkman gives away, it is said, fifteen quarts to the hundred "for good measure." This seems to be common experience. The writer of the letter sells over two hundred quarts per day, at six cents per quart, and claims that the jars save $2 for one day, and for 365 days over $700; or in ten years $7000.

THREE SIZES OF MILK BOTTLES.

Retail dairymen, especially if producers, do not usually measure closely. They commonly pour in a little extra milk. It is this extra milk, according to the above, that would pay for a good farm in ten years' time.

BOTTLE CARRIER.

The glass jar is a measure in itself. No extra milk goes with it. It protects both seller and buyer, and milk thus shipped commands a higher price. The bottles are of several sizes. The mouth is the same, in all cases, and is closed by the same circular bit of prepared pasteboard.

As the jars are filled when fresh everybody gets the same proportion of cream, which is right; and being full, there is no churning.

It is easy to estimate the quantity and quality of the bacteria which reach milk shipped in this excellent manner. They are few and harmless.

Who can compare the modern glass jar with the old-fashioned, big-mounted milk kettle that must be opened and closed a score of times in the dirty streets of a town or city, while the contents splash and churn from the moment the first dipperful is removed? Who can estimate the number of hostile bacteria which must of necessity get into milk so retailed, especially in summer weather?

The shipment of milk in glass jars will greatly tend to encourage its use. Milk is one of the best and cheapest of foods when in good order, but quite the reverse when improperly treated. Health is one result; bowel troubles the other.

I notice that the wholesale price of bottled milk in New York City the past summer (1897) has been one-half cent per quart higher than for milk shipped in bulk.

Butter quotations tell a story of their own. Butters known to the trade as "creameries" are divided into four grades, with just about a cent a pound between them. Going down the scale are the "imitation creameries," divided into three or four grades. The latter are genuine butter, but are of distinctly inferior quality. Then come the "special brands" of various sorts. In the quotations before me at this writing (quotations issued by one of the greatest firms in America) I find prices for these special brands even better than "creamery ex.," which heads the list just mentioned.

The moral is simple. It means that successful dairymen must get to the top of the market with a special brand. It is within reach of all who work for it. It is a matter of cleanliness, gumption and perseverance.

Quality being equal, a small parcel usually commands a higher price than a large parcel, for the simple reason that there are always more fifty-cent buyers than dollar buyers. Figure 1 shows a shipping crate containing 48 one-pound boxes of butter.

FIG. 1.

In the cheese quotations (on the same sheet with the butter quotations) I find the best prices are commanded by the full-cream brands which have made and kept good trade names.

It has been a hobby with me for some years (a theory, mind, not based on personal experience) that there is room in America for many varieties of cheese put up in small attractive packages. My cheese-making experience is not wide, as to varieties, but I see the eagerness with which the American public buys articles of food which appeal to its fancy. A quarter or half dollar is sure to be spent for a toothsome article which appeals to the eye as well as to palate.

The American dairyman must regard himself in more than one light. He is an individual engaged in money-earning work, for personal advantage, and he is also a part of a great public which is sometimes called "the Government," or "America." The efforts of the individual are necessarily limited in their scope, but when aggregated under the larger term it is possible to do great things.

There are good local markets for skimmilk, buttermilk, cottage cheese, etc., that can be developed by effort and good service. The local market is always worth having.

As to selling cream wholesale there is promise at this time of a general movement in America toward what is known as the cream-gathering system. This plan has grown up since the advent of the hand separator. It leaves all the by-products on the farm, removing only the cream, which is very low in fertility value. Hence the farm loses little or nothing, which is exceptional, as almost all agricultural products carry away much fertility with them.

Under the cream-gathering system the most satisfactory way of making settlements is for the central factory to pay a uniform price per pound in cash for actual butter fat.

CASH.

Wrong, all wrong, that the United States should export more bogus butter than real butter. Let's see to it.

The milk producer should net at least half the retail price, every time.

Poor butter paper molds the butter, and is a bad investment.

New and bright utensils always please buyers.

Many an article is sold by the neatness of its wrapper.

Cuts of Beef and Veal.

The United States Department of Agriculture has adopted the following terms for each of the different cuts of a butchered beef and veal.

1. Third cut neck.
2. Second cut neck.
3. First cut neck.
4. Third cut chuck ribs.
5. Second cut chuck ribs.
6. First cut chuck ribs.
7. Third cut ribs.
8. Second cut ribs.
9. First cut ribs.
10. Small end sirloin.
11. Hip sirloin.
12. Socket.
13. Rump.
14. First cut round.
15. Second cut round.
16. Leg.
17. Top of sirloin.
18. Flank.
19. Navel.
20. Plate.
21. Cross ribs.
22. Brisket.
23. Shin.
24. Brisket.

For Calves.

1. Neck.
2. Chuck.
3. Shoulders.
4. Fore shank.
5. Ribs.
6. Breast.
7. Loin.
8. Flank.
9. Hind shank.

Chapter XXI.

DAIRY APPLIANCES.

No more guesswork in the dairy.—John Tucker.

There is not a more useful and profitable thing than the Babcock tester in the entire range of dairy appliances. This instrument, or series of instruments, fills a long-felt dairy want, and, I think, does its work more accurately, quickly and cheaply than anything else of its kind on the market.

It is primarily useful in enabling the dairyman to know his cows and to accurately determine the cost of milk production. To the creamery man it is invaluable in the detection of waste, either in defective skimming or defective churning. There are several good testing systems on the market, including the so-called Leffman-Beam and the Cochran, but I will describe only the Babcock, because it is in widest American use at this time.

BABCOCK MILK TESTER.

Briefly, the Babcock test is an apparatus for determining the amount of butter fat in milk; or, it may be said, for determining the actual value of milk, because the value of milk depends on the total solids, and the total solids vary in amount as the fat varies in amount.

One chemical (sulphuric acid) is required, and the process demands only ten or fifteen minutes of time.

The cost per test is perhaps a quarter of a cent, and several tests can be made at once.

The process is not patented, and any dairyman is at liberty to use it, including the centrifugal or whirling machine required for its operation. The Babcock appliances are for sale at all dairy supply stores at reasonable prices.

Full and minute directions for operating the Babcock test are given in circulars sent out with the machine, and I need only describe the principle involved.

A given amount of milk is placed in a test glass and the same amount of sulphuric acid added to it. A milk test glass is shown Number 1, Figure 1. The solution takes on a dark coffee color, owing to the action of the acid on the milk sugar. The acid first precipitates the casein and then dissolves it. The fat is set free, and is not acted upon by the acid. Number 2, in Figure 1, shows the acid measure and Number 3 is the pipette for measuring the milk.

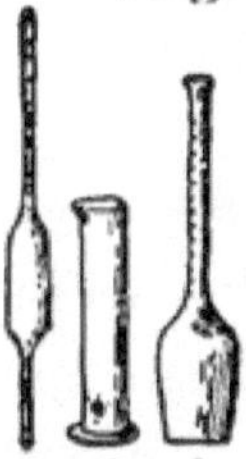

FIG. 1

The exact size of the test bottle is not important, but the size of the neck and the accuracy of the graduation marks are of vital importance. It is essential that precisely a given amount of milk be used in the sample bottle; that enough acid be used to liberate the fat; and that the amount of fat be accurately registered in the graduated neck of the bottle.

The acid having been added to the milk, and mixed therewith, the bottles are placed in the pockets of the centrifugal machine and whirled for about five minutes, at the rate of say 900 revolutions per minute. The fat is thus all collected.

In order to get the fat up into the tube, so as to be read, a little hot water is added, and the tube again whirled in the machine for a minute or two. The addition of this hot water will not affect the percentage, since the exact amount of milk is already known, and nothing remains except to get the fat into the accurately-marked neck.

It is not even necessary that the fat should begin at the zero mark in the tube. It can as well extend from 2 to 6 as from 0 to 4. In either case there would clearly be 4 per cent. of fat in the sample of milk.

Let it be understood that the neck of the test bottle (which is toward the centre of the whirling machine, when in motion) is so graduated as to accurately show percentage marks (of a milk sample weighing say 18 grams), regardless of the precise size of the bulb of the bottle.

These percentage spaces on the neck of the bottle are each subdivided into five parts, each of which represents one-fifth or two-tenths of one per cent.

Good skimming (gravity or separator) will take out all the butter fat from milk except about two-tenths of one per cent. In 100 pounds of 4 per cent. milk, yielding in theory 4 pounds of fat, this loss of two-tenths of one per cent. in skimming would amount to two-tenths of a pound of butter, or one-twentieth (5 per cent.) of the amount of butter fat in the whole milk. About as much is lost in churning, but the butter gains weight by carrying water, etc., with it in the final make-up.

In actual creamery practice tests are made of composite samples of each customer's milk; that is, of samples made day by day and kept in a jar, thus representing the average of a week or more.

A special bottle is used for testing skimmilk. It has a side tube for the addition of the acid (a mere convenience), and the graduated neck is much smaller than in ordinary test bottles. This is done to make small amounts of fat more accurately read.

A so-called "oil test churn," for determining the butter value of cream collected in the cream-gathering system of operating a butter factory, is now offered for sale.

In this book I cannot mention even by name the thousand and one conveniences now on the market. It is not my purpose to write a catalogue for a dairy supply house, but rather to tell how to read a catalogue.

MILK STRAINER.

Beginning with the milk strainer, I must call attention to a device in which the milk flow is upward instead of downward through the gauze. There are two gauzes or screens, and I like this implement because it avoids pouring the milk directly upon the sediment arrested by the strainer.

PATENT STRAINER.

As to a milk cooler, I have already urged the choice of the one doing the work well and which can be *most easily cleaned.* This is equivalent to an endorsement of a cooler where the milk runs over an exposed cold surface, rather than through cold pipes. The objection to the former style is that the milk may absorb bacteria from the air with which it comes so freely in contact, but this merely necessitates a cleanly atmosphere, apart from the cow stable. An exterior surface may be made clean, but the inside of a pipe is always liable to suspicion.

The separator is now thoroughly established in American dairying, and several rival machines are upon the market. If we may believe the advertisements published by the owners of these separators it must be concluded that some of them are far less efficient than others. But if we may believe the testimony of the experiment station experts it is safe to buy any of them.

The power separator has already worked a great change in American dairying, as shown by the establishment of thousands of creameries in the United States.

The hand separator seems likely to work another change, almost as universal, as indicated in the growth of what is called the cream-gathering system. By the latter plan only the cream goes to the factory, instead of the whole milk as formerly.

As to hand separators, I am quite willing to accept the verdict of the Pennsylvania station, to the effect that the trials (ending March 20, 1897) showed very little if any difference in completeness of skimming and total amount of fat recovered in the cream. Considerable difference was noted, however, in ease of operation and apparent durability of the several machines tested. No difference in character of cream was found, and the conclusion was reached

HAND SEPARATOR.

that the choice of a hand separator should depend largely on first cost and apparent durability.

It is held by some dairymen that a separator pays with seven cows.

There are several patterns of glass jars or bottles for the shipment of milk now upon the market, some with temporary and some with permanent tops or lids. They are made in at least four sizes, from half pints up to half gallons. The bottle which most forcibly commends itself to me, from personal observation, is the one with a pasteboard (or pulp) top; the top to be used but once. This top is water-proof and prevents the milk from spilling, and also prevents dust from entering the bottle.

There is a device for rapidly filling these comparatively small milk vessels; and wire baskets are made for carrying them. Boxes are provided for packing in ice, so that the jars may be kept cool for a long time, and a foot-power washer has been

BOTTLE FILLER. constructed to facilitate quick and thorough cleansing of the returned vessels.

Here is a cream stirrer good for putting the cream in the right condition for making gilt-edge butter. The bottom is from six to eight inches across, and the top two to three inches. It may be five to six inches high. A No. 9 wire, galvanized, is used for a handle, with which to push the mixer down and to lift it up in the mess of cream. The effect is to stir the cream and aerate it from the bottom to the top and to mix it most thoroughly.

Ice tubs for holding cans of cream are sold by the dealers in dairy supplies. The cream from such cans reaches the consumer in a highly attractive and palatable condition.

I mention this merely to emphasize the fact that the retail trade (the best way to sell, where possible) is influenced almost wholly by little details of this kind. People buy what pleases them.

It is impossible to enumerate the tin vessels used by dairymen, for these vessels are legion. I examine the catalogues with great interest, and frequently get useful ideas from these publications. Sometimes I can buy articles cheaper and better a thousand miles from home than in the city nearest to me; and these catalogues tell me what other dairymen demand. Of course every article in the many-paged catalogue represents somebody's thought and experience.

A handy thing in any dairy is a good circulating boiler for hot water as shown in the illustration.

It was a good idea, for instance, for me to buy some large, plainly-printed signs of "buttermilk," "cottage cheese," "fresh butter," etc., which were mentioned in one of the catalogues. They cost me but a few cents, and increased my sales in market.

Another thing, first seen in the catalogues, was the convenient "milk sack," made of water-proof manilla paper. I use them for retailing the above products, including skimmilk, to people who would otherwise go past my stall on account of having neither kettles nor pitchers with them.

There is a milk-can jacket advertised for the prevention of freezing in cold weather; a "power," especially built for bulls, to run the separator; a low-priced steamer or boiler, for steaming feeds; and a small and cheap boiler and engine. These things, once to be had only of various dealers (or not at all), can now be found in all the dairy supply stores.

Finally, as to dairy cleanliness, let me advise washing, scalding, rinsing and sunning, in the order named. Dairy implements, of all things, must be kept sweet.

ORDERLIES.

Sunlight and fresh air and hot water are the cardinal factors in cleanliness.

The odor of whitewash is the only allowable smell in milk house or creamery.

There are many good butter workers on the market. Buy that one which has greatest simplicity. Keep it clean.

Printing butter is as much of an art as stamping gold coins.

It is a great help in keeping a cow clean in the stable to shear off the long hairs of her tail.

Getting milk frozen hauling it to the creameries is one cause of poor butter. On very cold days the cans should be covered on the way to the creamery.

Sunlight is death to bacteria.

When limited cash compels a dairy owner to do his own work, instead of hiring it done, it is generally well done.

Keep things clean on the outside of the creamery. Ill odors tell of lost fertility.

The milk wagon is an advertisement on wheels. Make it attractive.

In all the range of household work no occupation is more graceful for girls than butter making.

Neat prints will add ten per cent. to the price of butter. Most manufacturers think ten per cent. a big profit.

One of the standard doctrines of modern dairy practice is that disinfectants can never take the place of simple old-fashioned cleanliness.

Have you tried clipping the hair from the hind legs of the cows so they won't get clogged with dung?

Chapter XXII.

THE PUBLIC CREAMERY.

Don't hurry the cows and then waste time at the creamery.—
                                              John Tucker.

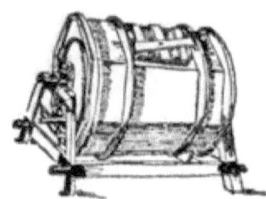
POWER CHURN.

A public creamery should be a public convenience, saving much drudgery. Managed properly, it may be profitable, a good thing in many ways for the community. Success depends wholly upon an abundance of cream and judicious management. Any town may have a prosperous creamery if resident men of average ability can be interested and at least 400 good cows absolutely pledged. The risks in the business have been lessened greatly by the Babcock system, the manager paying for only the fats he can make into a salable article. No creamery can be run on a permanent basis of profit without the Babcock test or some method equally reliable. All dangers to the life of the enterprise have not been removed and never can be. Tact in management is priceless. There are still many sharks to avoid, who would wreck the owner or the organization in building, in equipping, or in both together, or in receiving consignments and making inadequate returns or none. Many creameries have been fitted up at $5000 to $8000 that should not have cost over $3000 to $4500. And of course any concern expected to pay reasonable dividends upon twice as

A MODEL NEW HAMPSHIRE CREAMERY.

much stock as necessary could make but a poor showing; the patrons would get dissatisfied and withdraw, making the supply of milk inadequate, and forcing operations to stop. A creamery closed is hard to reopen, as the confidence of the public must be regained.

Any individual or association of farmers convinced that a creamery can be added safely and profitably to the institutions of the place, should not inaugurate one hastily. A careful canvass should be made to ascertain how many dairies there are whose owners will pledge themselves in writing to furnish milk from a stated number of cows the first year. Any grants of land, material and labor that public-spirited citizens may make should be received gratefully.

Sometimes stockholders desire to pay for stock in this way which they could not own otherwise. Experience proves that the best way is not to place the contract for building and equipping with some concern making a specialty of such things but to hire local carpenters and masons of good repute under contracts with carefully drawn plans and specifications and to buy the boiler, engine, tanks, separators, pipes, valves, etc., where they can be secured to the best advantage, quality considered. An equipment second-hand and nearly new is offered frequently at a price that will make its acceptance profitable.

Location is everything in keeping down labor bills, for an unhandy creamery or one too large or too small will require an extra hand, and here is a big leak in good management. Location influences quality largely, and only butter of finest flavor brings the highest price. Since strictest cleanliness is essential, it is obvious that the creamery must not stand in a swamp, nor where good drainage is not feasible. Wash water or milk if not carried completely away will pollute the air in three days. If the creamery is situated so large quantities of milk may be received and handled with little effort on the part of the help, the milk running by its own weight from the receiving room through strainers, vats, separators, and again into the owners' wagons, without pumping or lifting, much is gained. Site, plan, equipment, locating just right upon the site—all these should be studied for months and many other plants visited before a stick or brick is bought, or any contract given. A studious contemplation of and comparison with other creameries often reveal defects that may be remedied easily in the plan before it is executed. A large plant, suited to handling the milk from 1200 to 1500 cows, erected after such careful consideration, is shown. It is run partly upon the whole milk and partly upon the gathered plan and is a success. The whole milk plan makes each dairy send its milk to the creamery or to one of its separating stations at a stated time, usually once per day, and is in wide use in the West, while but little practised in the East. In the gathering plan followed east and west the creamery sends teams to collect the cream which is raised on the farm by some system of setting or by hand separators. There is but little difference in the methods followed east and west, the old principle of cleanliness recognized by our forefathers and mothers being considered the great secret of success everywhere.

The creamery whose plan is shown here is 30 x 60 feet, built in a side hill and the system of gravity used from start to finish. The whole milk that is received is weighed in on the top floor, not shown, heated, and piped down, down and out. A, is the fuel house; B, the office; C, the ice house, 20 x 20 feet and 26 feet deep, holding 200 tons; D, a cool room adjoining the cooler E; F, windows; G, doors; H, a pier running out to load butter and cream from; 1, is the engine; 2, boiler; 3, separators; 4, cream cooler; 5, Babcock tester, the line shaft shown crossing it is 10 feet above it; 6, steps to the half story where separators and

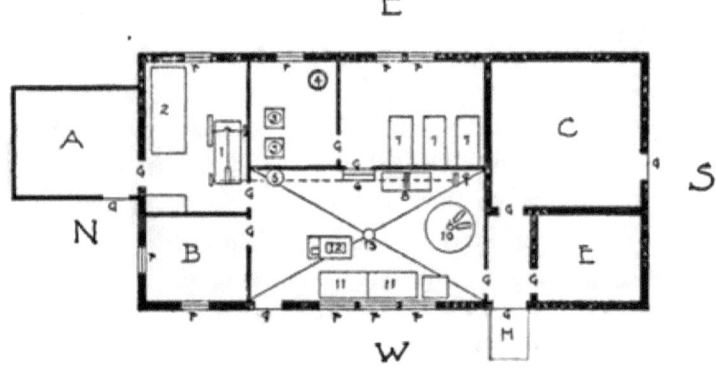

·PLAN·OF·CREAMERY·

cream vats 7 are kept; 8, is 300 gallon box churn into which cream is run from vats; 9, pulley to run butter worker 10; 11, sink; 12, pasteurizing outfit; 13, drain to which everything falling on work room floor runs. Another drain catches the buttermilk let out of the churn and leads it to a distance where it is put into barrels on a wagon and finds its way to a large piggery.

Eastern or New England creameries market their butter direct to stores and hotels, sending by express in single cases at a time, mostly in pound prints wrapped in parchment, instead of through commission houses, as western creameries do.

A large supply of cold sweet water is among essentials. Prosperous creamery managers everywhere have learned the importance of securing and retaining a buttermaker of highest ability, faithfulness and integrity.

Rigid rules should be adopted for the government of patrons in their management of stables, cows and milk. The following are excellent :

Cows should be driven quietly and treated gently for best results, should have pure water in abundance and none that is stagnant.

Salt regularly. Udders should be washed often.

Milk should be aired immediately by pouring or dipping and then cooled as quickly as possibly to 60° or lower.

No morning's milk should be mixed with night's milk until chilled.

Pails and cans should be washed with warm, not hot, water to get all milk from the seams and then scalded.

Milkers never should milk with wet hands.

Other rules may be added suited to the locality adopting these.

GOSSIP.

Dairying requires the strength of a man and the patience of a woman.

Skimmilk should be kept on the farm ; not given away.

The Thomas Parker Creamery, of Lawrence, Kansas, is one of many similar large plants. It has 27 skimming stations, and a cream car with its attendant makes daily collections, testing the cream en route. The great St. Albans, Vt., creamery runs 67 separators and gathers mostly by rail.

The Babcock test has routed the unjust payment by space and the old pooling of milk plan. It pays for the actual fat in the milk, and careful breeding and wise feeding are encouraged.

Chapter XXIII.

VILLAGER'S ONE COW.

With a good cow and a good kitchen garden any family is rich.—Dorothy.

The keeper of one cow or two cows cares but little for the chemistry of feeds or the arithmetic of dairying, but is interested mainly in getting the most and best milk for the least money. I will therefore present a few rations without fully discussing their make-up.

Pasture grass is the summer mainstay of the one-cow dairy, and pasture grass is an almost perfect cow food. The grass is usually supplemented with a little bran and corn meal. Bran is rich in protein, which goes direct to the milk pail; corn meal is more apt to lodge on the ribs in the form of fat.

All the edible waste from the kitchen should go to cow, pig or chickens; and if pigs or chickens are not kept the cow will do much toward saving the waste of good food. She will eat many vegetables, either cooked or raw; and even skimmilk may be used to advantage in her feed box, upon cut feed of any kind.

The waste from the garden, including all cornstalks, makes good cow feed; and the mowings of the yard can be advantageously disposed of in the same way. The family cow can be petted and pampered in a manner quite impossible with a herd, and with highly satisfactory results.

If there is room to pasture the cow, so much the better. Otherwise an amazing amount of succulent fodder can be produced on a few square rods of ground, and cut as required. Always grow roots, such as mangels and sugar beets. Pumpkins are excellent. Cabbages, turnips and such things may be fed in moderation, after milking.

No one has any right to allow stock to run at large. No one is obliged to fence stock out of, or off their lands. Every one is liable for all damages their animals do, if allowed to run at large, or for trespass upon others' lands. Animals must be guarded or fenced in upon their owner's lands. This is common law. In New York State road fences are being taken up, and the grounds about dwellings are not enclosed. This saves money and adds to the appearance of the farms.

MINDING THE ROADSIDE COW.

A cow consumes of good hay (or its equivalent) about 3 per cent. of her live weight daily; or, in other terms, the ration should include say 2 pounds of coarse, bulky food (hay, fodder, etc.) and 1 pound of grain per day per 100 pounds of weight of cow.

I would use twice as much bran as corn meal (by weight) in making up a ration for a cow in milk. Of course the corn meal would be necessary in larger proportion in fattening an animal.

The family cow varies a good deal in weight.

Perhaps 1000 pounds would not be much above the American average, and the ration may be figured accordingly. Here is a winter ration, to be divided and used so as to cover a day:

>15 pounds clover hay,
>10   "   wheat bran,
>5   "   corn meal.
>(Nutritive ratio about 1: 5.6).

This is a good ration, but not the cheapest. It may be supplemented with a few chopped sugar beets or other roots, or with chopped pumpkins or apples. The private dairyman as a rule does not have access to ensilage, which yields succulent food where large herds are to be supplied.

It does not require a big milker to average 10 quarts per day for six months and 5 quarts per day for four months. This makes a total of say 5160 pounds and gives the cow a resting period of eight weeks.

The one-cow dairyman must continue to depend on the shallow pan system of setting milk; a very good plan where things are kept clean.

As to churning, I say churn often. Churn three times a week for the best butter. Churn twice a week for good butter. Ripen the cream at least 24 hours; then churn at a temperature of 65° in winter or 60° in summer. Much is lost by allowing cream to stand after it is ripe. An egg beater will answer for churning a small amount of cream.

THIS KIND.

The so-called grade or part thoroughbred is an ideal family cow. My preference includes some of the

Channel Islands blood, blended with any other good stock.

Cows appreciate kindness, and will repay it. A good grooming will sometimes be quickly followed by an increased milk flow.

A fly sheet on the family cow will add to her comfort, and tend to larger productiveness and more desirable milk for family use.

Here is a plan of a village barn suitable for a horse, cow and carriage. It is about 20 feet square, and the shed attached 12 x 20. The floor shown through the open door gives ample room for carriages, sleigh, the lawn mower, etc., besides room to unhitch, and clean harness. The harness closet is on the barn floor near the vehicles where no ammonia from the stables can reach it. The horse can be taken from the floor directly into the stable without going out of doors.

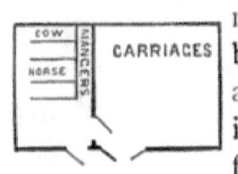

GENTLENESS.

The dewlap is that hanging portion of the neck which during grazing "laps the dew."

Always have fodder corn in midsummer.

No animal responds to good treatment so quickly as the cow. Favors are acknowledged in terms of milk.

The villager's cow must be quiet and docile.

Teach the cow to submit to a halter, and to follow easily when led.

The lone cow often bellows for water. Keep her quiet by supplying her reasonable needs.

Some cows are permanently discontented when alone. Such animals do best in herds.

Never touch the butter with the hands.

Chapter XXIV.

THE MILK FARM.

Give all the clover possible.—John Tucker.

THE OLD SPRING HOUSE.

My object in conducting a milk farm is to make money; not merely to work out new theories of dairy practice. Still, I must confess to more than one change of method within the past quarter century, on account of altered commercial conditions. My fundamental rule is to grow nearly everything at home, and to sell off the least possible amount of fertility. The farm is the source of raw materials, the dairy is the factory where goods are made up, the cows are the laborers, and I am the business manager. Of course I never hesitate to sell farm produce when prices are good, for then I can buy artificial manures. But my main reliance for fertility is the covered manure shed, where all manure is piled up in neat and compact form.

My cows are all home-raised; not that this plan is so much cheaper, but because it is so much more satisfactory than any other. There is a deal of pleasure in shaping the career of a heifer calf two or more generations in advance of her birth; and I have animals where three generations pasture side by side and vie with each other in the dairy—with the grand-daughters leading. I try to breed for winter milkers.

Dehorning is practised. A little caustic on the calf's head nips the horns in the bud. Some day, no doubt, polled, or hornless bulls, will be relied upon for the dehorning process. I read that a Galloway bull will get hornless calves 99 times out of 100, from horned cows; but I use a lighter-built bull in my herd of milk cows, and such bulls have horns. If the feeling against horned cows continue, we shall presently hear of polled Jerseys and polled Guernseys; but such strains are not yet in the market. The only objection to dehorning that I have yet heard (outside of the operation itself)

A CORNER OF A MILK FARM.

is that hornless cows crowd together too closely in the pasture field, and may suffer from overheating on very sultry days in summer.

I rely mainly on timothy, clover, Kentucky blue grass and corn fodder; but of course I have accepted the silo and ensilage. And I am quite sure that crimson clover has come to stay as far north as southern Pennsylvania, and that other leguminous plants must be recognized in our farm and dairy calculations.

I make no violent or sudden changes in my farming operations, but shall be wide awake to what other dairymen are doing in the way of growing leguminous plants either for feeding, for ensilage, or for green manuring. If pea vines and vetches are really worth as much as the concentrated mill feeds, I propose to save part of the feed bills.

Improvement can assuredly be made in our pasture lands, both in preparation of the soil and in choice of grass seeds. The soil preparation should involve some manuring (as much as possible) and a greater variety of grasses. Different grasses mature at different dates, and the season of good grazing can be prolonged by a wise choice of seeds. For a grazing field for cows, in addition to the usual timothy and red clover, I use Kentucky blue grass, herd's-grass, and white clover.

It may be urged that some of these things come of themselves, but I sow them when the ground is prepared. It pays. Indeed, it will pay to sow grass seeds without a grain crop of any kind, on manured soil. Alfalfa does quite well where the subsoil is porous. It is a clover in fact. I sow corn for summer soiling; also millet.

The milk farm should produce roots for stock feeding, especially where ensilage is not used. Sugar beets and mangels are desirable, and when sown in rows and well cultivated by horse power an enormous tonnage per acre may be harvested. Turnips, rutabagas and carrots are also desirable adjuncts to the rations of a stall-fed cow; five to ten pounds per day per head is a sufficient amount of roots. Mangels should be ripened by storage before being fed. Apples, potatoes, pumpkins, etc., also have a place in the autumn and winter ration, and are excellent when fed in moderation and with good judgment. Corn fodder should be housed or else compactly stacked near the barn; otherwise it is injured by the weather. Dairymen must learn to balance their own cow rations from the feeds at their command.

MILK TALK.

There's money in the pea plant and its allies—the beans, tares and vetches. Clover is in close kinship too.

Grow all the clover possible.

Eighty per cent. of the manurial value of foods is returned in the manure. Take care of it.

Cows with leaky teats should be milked three times a day.

It is poor policy to teach a cow to let her milk down only when being fed.

Throw a ripped-open fertilizer bag over a fly-teased cow at milking time.

Many a man has made many a penny by combining calf with skimmilk.

Keep the cow's fly brush clean.

Pure water, not tainted water, for the cow's beverage.

Remember the salt. Use a little powdered sulphur, too, when salting the young stock.

If a cow is not a deep drinker she cannot be a deep milker.

Never before has so much been expected of the cow. Now she will not pass muster with a high test and a long pedigree. She must give also a fair quantity and be an all-the-year-round milker.

The day has gone by when it is considered cheaper to buy a cow than to raise one. Not that there are not cows (things) for sale, but the thinking dairyman knows how hard it is to find profitable cows, even at ruinous prices.

The output of choice butter and cheese is enormous, but the demand for it is still more enormous, and on the increase. Lucky the man who can lead in quality or in a choice specialty.

To know how to get the largest cash return from home grown stuff, usually roughage, by combining it with the right kind and quantity of bought foods, is to know how to make the dairy pay.

Milk is wasted at the rate of half a pint to a quart per cow by some milkers because they fail to hold the pail properly while milking. The loss occurring twice daily is a big one in a year.

Chapter XXV.

AILMENTS AND REMEDIES.

Good care is the farmer's best cow doctor.—Dorothy.

Let sick or maimed animals lie still. Do not torture them by trying to get them up. Rub their limbs every day and keep a soft bed under them. They will get up when they are able.

If a cow look poor and weak, put a blanket on her, keep her in a warm place, and feed her some corn meal and middlings, and some oats. Give her warm drink, and stir a little cheap flour in it. Do not let her run clear down. Look ahead.

If cows are accidentally left out in a rain and seem cold, put them in the stable as soon as possible and rub them well. If they shiver, put blankets on them until they are dry. If there is inflammation or hardness in the udder, bathe it thoroughly for at least half an hour, and rub gently until thoroughly dry.

If this does not effect a cure put a *warm* flaxseed poultice on the udder, which can be held in place by means of an eight-tailed bandage. This should be changed twice a day until the hardness and soreness are gone. Of course, the cow should be milked out two or three times each day.

Now I will speak of some vices and their cure. Vicious bulls are generally rendered civil by dehorning. A ring in the nose is sufficient in some animals. To put ring in nose secure the animal by tying securely by a rope around the horns. With a sharp knife or large sack needle puncture the membrane between the nostrils and insert the ring. A few links of heavy chain fastened to the ring by a spring hook is useful in very bad animals.

To keep bulls from injuring or killing persons, in place of dehorning fix a blind over the eyes, of stout, heavy leather, attached to a head halter. It will make the animal comparatively harmless. The same plan will prevent fence-breaking in any of the cattle kind. See that the fastening does not cut the skin around the horns. It may be said that dehorning will quite answer, but this is a mistake. Watch the muley bull.

THE BREACHY COW.

Or fasten a light but strong stick or slat from tip to tip of horns. A strip of oak or hickory, or other tough wood, one and a quarter inches thick, one and three-quarters to two inches wide and two inches longer than the extreme width of horns is all sufficient. Bore holes in the end to admit the tips of the horns and fasten on with screws, and the job is complete.

A cow that sucks herself is a bother. She may be prevented doing so by a necklace made from old broom or fork handles, strung on a strap and buckled around the neck. It should be fitted to the cow and the sticks made long enough to keep her from putting her head on her side and not long enough to chafe the shoulders or throat when the head is not turned; or a hollow bit may be used; or a wide leather around the nose filled with sharp nails pointing outward. Sew on a strap to buckle over the top of the head.

Cows become kickers through training, not by inherent badness. A strap placed as in the picture and buckled tight will stop her kicking. A kicker is not benefited by cruelty; try kind treatment; if it fail, try again.

If cows are found gnawing bones in the pasture when they should be eating grass or chewing the cud, it shows that something is wrong with the herd or the pasture.

Steers and dry cows rarely acquire the habit, and it is more common in extra good than in poor milkers. It usually prevails where cows have been kept in the same pasture many years by day and taken out nights. It may not be cured at once by changing to richer feed, but I have never known cows to chew bones very long after being given abundant rations of wheat bran and clover hay, or other food containing abundant proportions of bone-making material which the milk must have.

If cows are not fed a variety of food they will eat horse manure to get the salts out of it. In the horse manure are soda, magnesia, salt, phosphoric acid, potash, nitrogen and lime. Give such cows bran, salt and fine meal.

OF DEHORNING.

This may be done at any age, but best done as soon as the horn buttons are perceptible, by touching the young horn and surrounding skin with a stick of caustic potash. Wrap the caustic stick with paper to protect the fingers, moisten the unwrapped end with water and apply to a circular spot not larger than a silver quarter dollar. Vinegar is a good antidote to caustic potash and should be applied at once to hands or any part of skin accidentally touched.

Young horns may also be removed by strong knife before the horn becomes tightly fastened. Make a circular cut around the horn, then cut well beneath it and lift the young horn out.

Horns of adult cattle may be removed by a sharp saw, but the dehorning implements now in the market are much better. The advantages of dehorning are that the animals become more docile, the timid ones in the herd are not annoyed, and cruelty is not practised upon one another.

OF THE DIGESTIVE ORGANS.

If a cow get a foreign body in the mouth turn her head towards the light and remove it.

For CHOKING, examine throat and neck; if offending object is felt, attempt to force upward into the mouth by pressure of hands below the object. Give one pint linseed oil or melted lard. May sometimes reach with hand by holding tongue aside. Do not push a stiff stick or fork handle down the throat; a piece of rubber hose, well greased, is less likely to ruin the cow.

If a cow has BLOAT or HOVEN there will be a drum-like swelling on left side in front of hip, caused by green food, wet or frosted clover, overfeeding, choking. Give one-half teacupful table salt in water, as drench. Exercise. If not relieved give aromatic spirits of ammonia, two ounces, well diluted, every hour. Where there is great danger of suffocation a puncture of the paunch may be made with a knife or better yet by an instrument here shown (Fig. 1.), the trocar and canula. It consists of a sharp blade in a tube about half an inch in diameter and eight inches long. When the puncture is made the trocar is withdrawn and the tube remains, allowing the gas to escape. Figure 2 shows the point, equally distant from the point of the hip and the last rib, where the puncture should be made.

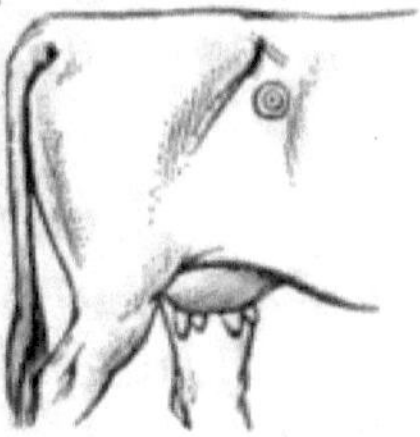

FIG. 1.

FIG. 2.

IMPACTION OF PAUNCH is caused by overeating, and the symptoms are failing appetite, solid or doughy swelling on front of left hip. Give one to two pounds Glauber salts dissolved in water; follow every three hours by drench of mixture of equal parts common salt, nux vomica powdered and capsicum. Dose, one tablespoonful.

In COLIC the symptoms are uneasiness, striking belly with hind legs, lying down and getting up. Cause, change of diet, rapid feeding. Give Glauber salts, one pound in water; warm water enemas. Give every hour one ounce each of laudanum and sulphuric ether, diluted.

CONSTIPATION caused by dry, coarser food and lack of exercise, is treated with green food, linseed meal and exercise; give pint of raw linseed oil. DIARRHŒA is treated with starch gruel or flour and water and dry food.

SCOURS in calves is caused by overfeeding, bad food or drink, damp stables, dirty surroundings. Remove cause and withhold food the best remedy. Give once daily twenty grains potassium permanganate in tincup of water; also use same for enema.

Cows are subject to FOUNDER, showing sudden tenderness in two or more feet; feet hot and may crack around top of hoof. This comes from overfeeding. Give Glauber salts one pound, twenty drops tincture aconite every two hours. Keep feet moist by wet pasture or wet cloths.

GARGET or SWOLLEN UDDER, due to cold, injuries, overfeeding or heating food. Bathe frequently with warm water; dry, and apply warm lard. Milk often. Give internally two-drachm doses salicylic acid and one drachm soda bicarbonate in one pint of milk four times daily.

OF THE BREATHING ORGANS.

DISCHARGE OF MUCUS from nostrils indicates catarrh from exposure, dust, or pollen of plants. Allow animal to breathe steam from water containing pine tar.

In SORE THROAT there is difficulty in swallowing, food returns through nostrils. Steam as in catarrh, give tincture belladonna one-half ounce every six hours. Rub throat with equal parts turpentine and sweet oil.

In BRONCHITIS there is dry cough first, then loose, and discharge from nostrils; rattling sound in windpipe. Steam as in sore throat and give tincture aconite twenty drops every two hours and two drachms muriate ammonia in one pint of water three times daily. For bronchitis in young stock due to worms in windpipe, which sometimes occur in autumn where they are pastured late, give one ounce turpentine and six ounces sweet oil well mixed, three times a week. Take from pasture and feed liberally.

In Pneumonia there is loss of appetite, animal standing, rapid breathing, pulse frequent, extremities cold. Cause, exposure or neglected bronchitis. Place in a warm, dry, well-ventilated stable, apply to chest equal parts turpentine and alcohol and cover with blanket. In beginning give tincture aconite twenty drops every hour. If not better in two days discontinue aconite and give one ounce tr. digitalis every eight hours.

In Pleurisy there is fever with rapid pulse, animal stands, grunts on moving or when chest is struck, has a short painful cough. Treat same as for pneumonia; give also one drachm iodide of potash twice daily.

OF THE SKIN.

Sore Teats are caused by scratches from briers, bites of insects, dirt, exposure, also from the contagion of cow pox at milking. Remove cause and use milk tube if necessary; apply to sores after milking small quantity of mixture glycerine four ounces and carbolic acid one drachm. In cow pox milk affected cow last and apply to sores mixture glycerine four ounces, water eight ounces, chloride of zinc twenty grains.

Warts on teats or other parts are generally easily removed by sharp scissors; dress wound as advised for sore teats.

Mange causes great itching and generally starts at root of tail or top of neck; cause, a minute parasite. Wash with soap and water and dry, after which apply lard which destroys the parasite.

For Lice and Ticks apply daily a tea made by adding one pound quassia chips to three gallons of boiling water. Ordinary sheep dip is also effective. Carbolic acid is one of the most effective agents against parasites. It should have a dilution of about one hundred times its bulk of water. Kerosene emulsion is good for lice on cattle, killing both adults and eggs. To make, dissolve one-half pound hard soap in one gallon hot water and while still near the boiling point add two gallons kerosene oil. Churn or agitate until emulsified. Use one part of this emulsion to eight or ten parts of water and use as a spray, wash or dip.

In Ringworm there are circular spots of baldness covered by gray or yellow crust; caused also by a parasite. Wash with strong soap and water and apply pure creolin once daily for a week.

Foul Claw or Hoof Distemper causes lameness in one or more feet, swelling and heat around top of hoof, and bad smelling discharge around edge of hoof and between the claws. Cause, dirty stables, standing in stagnant water or mud. Trim off all loose horn, clean by wiping with dry rags, wet sores twice daily with mixture chloride of zinc one ounce, water one pint.

OVERGROWTH OF HOOF from standing in stable should be filed off with rasp.

OF VARIOUS INJURIES.

When chaff or other dirt gets into the eye syringe or sponge the eye frequently with clean cold water containing sulphate of zinc one grain to each ounce of water. Keep stable darkened.

SPRAINS (generally below knee or hock), causing heat and lameness with tenderness at point of injury, should be bathed with warm water or with laudanum three parts, lead water one part.

WOUNDS, if bleeding much, fill or cover the wound with clean cotton dipped in cold or quite warm water, and secure firmly with bandage; examine for foreign bodies, as splinters, nails and dirt. Do not fill wound with cobwebs to stop bleeding. Remove the bandage before swelling takes place; one application of bandage usually enough. Keep animal quiet first day, then allow exercise. Keep wound clear and apply carbolic acid water 5 per cent. or creolin and water 1 to 10. Do not apply grease to wounds. If proud flesh forms apply daily enough powdered burnt alum to cover.

For an ABSCESS or cavity containing pus caused by bruises, etc., open freely and syringe with 10 per cent. creolin solution.

LOCKJAW, a constant muscular spasm involving more or less the entire body, is caused by the entrance of tetanus germs through a wound. There is stiffness of whole or part of body, more frequently the jaws, making eating difficult or impossible. If animal can drink give one-half ounce doses bromide potash five times daily; dissolve and place on food or gruel or in water given to drink. Do not drench, and keep quiet.

OF THE GENERATIVE ORGANS.

INVERSION OF VAGINA most frequent in springers, caused most frequently by stalls too low behind. Treat displaced parts with warm water and replace them. Place cow in stall eight inches higher behind than in front until after calving.

INVERSION OF WOMB occurs after calving, same cause as above and treatment the same; get womb placed well forward.

STERILITY in bull is sometimes caused by high feeding and lack of exercise. Give nux vomica one drachm and capsicum one-half drachm once daily. In cow may be temporary, following abortion; if from other cause, seldom recover. Try same remedy as for bull.

ABORTION is a frequent and troublesome malady, occurring generally at about seventh or eighth month. Cause may be due to injuries or to contagion. Separate at once when suspected; after calf is born syringe the womb with one gallon warm water containing one ounce creolin. Repeat daily as long as any discharge is seen. Afterbirth should be removed about third day after calving. Disinfect stables thoroughly. Do not let cow take bull for at least two months after aborting.

RETAINED AFTERBIRTH is generally due to premature birth; should be removed on third or fourth day. Blanketing, warm stable, warm drinks may help. If necessary to remove by hand, should only be attempted by qualified person, otherwise it is advisable to allow it to remain.

INFLAMMATION OF THE WOMB is indicated by fever, loss of appetite, straining. Caused by injuries in calving or to attempts at removal of afterbirth, and is generally fatal. Give two drachms salicylate of soda every four hours and syringe womb with warm water and two ounces creolin to the gallon.

MILK FEVER or PARTURIENT APOPLEXY, a disease peculiar to cows, appearing not later than three days after calving, never occurring after first calving, and rarely before third. The cow is weak and staggers when moved and goes down unable to rise, appetite fails, the head is thrown to one side and rests with nose on the ground; bowels do not act—she may become totally unconscious, breathing first slow, becoming more rapid. Preventive treatment is best, exercise, laxative food, prevent excessive fattening, give one pound Glauber salts if necessary to keep bowels loose; give good box stall for calving; avoid cold air and water before and after calving, milk before calving if bag be distended. If disease develops give at once one and one-half pounds Glauber salts dissolved in hot water, also warm water enemas. Keep cow propped on breast by bundles of straw, cover body with blanket, apply cold water or ice bag to the head. Give every two hours two ounces each of aromatic spirits of ammonia and sweet spirits of nitre in cold water. Use great care in drenching; the throat being

AILMENTS AND REMEDIES.   139

more or less paralyzed, choking is likely to occur. She should be turned often and milked.

OF SOME OTHER SERIOUS MALADIES.

TUBERCULOSIS—Consumption is a contagious disease caused by a germ called "Bacillus Tuberculosis." The symptoms are not well marked in early stages; advanced cases show loss of flesh, a short, dry cough, diarrhœa, irregular appetite, enlargements about throat, head or in udder, and also symptoms of bronchitis, pleurisy and pneumonia when these diseases frequently become complications. Generally requires months or even years to destroy the victims; all the while the patient may communicate the disease to other animals and to man. This disease can be detected in its earliest stages by injection of tuberculin, after which the temperature in the affected animal is elevated. The test is very delicate and trustworthy in experienced hands. There being no known cure for tuberculosis, and the products of diseased animals being unsafe to use, the true course is to first apply the tuberculin test, which is done by many states without expense to the owner, and diseased cattle killed and paid for; and second, thoroughly disinfect stables to prevent reappearance.

ACTINOMYCOSIS (LUMP JAW) is a contagious disease due to a germ known as "Ray fungus." There are well-defined swellings about the jaw, head and throat, or may be on the tongue or in the lungs. These soften and open after a time and discharge matter; appetite good until well advanced. The treatment is, remove by surgical means; late experiments indicate iodide of potash two to three drachms daily to be a cure. Advanced cases should be killed at once. The meat should never be used for food.

MILK SICKNESS (TREMBLES) is a disease of cattle communicable to man and other animals by use of meat or milk; dry cattle most commonly and far more severely affected. Milch cows may transmit this disease through the use of their milk and yet show no trace of the disease themselves. The symptoms are trembling upon least exertion as walking, great prostration and delirium. Treatment is only prevention; do not use pastures known to produce this disease; unbroken land of certain districts unsafe.

RHEUMATISM is shown by hot, painful swellings at the joints, generally the hocks, stiffness in walking or may be unable to rise. Bathe joints with camphor and alcohol and give internally two drachms salicylate of soda every three hours until four ounces have been given; keep warm and dry and give laxative food.

TEXAS FEVER, a disease of southern cattle which, when transmitted to northern cattle, is generally fatal in a few days. The spread of the disease is generally due to ticks; those from diseased animals contain the germs of the disease and by their bites transmit it. The indications are a high fever, staggering gait, urine of reddish brown to black, great prostration, unconsciousness, death. Most common in summer months; unknown in the north after heavy frost. Prevention, avoidance of cattle from southern fever districts; dipping of southern cattle to destroy the ticks.

POINTERS ON DISINFECTION.

The germs of disease are so small that only the most complete methods will render an infected building safe.

Remove all litter, dirt and dust from floor, ceiling and walls.

Old wood-work, as troughs, racks and flooring had better be replaced by new.

All wood-work allowed to remain should be scrubbed at least three times with *hot* water and washing soda.

After each washing apply with whitewash brush or, better, a spray pump, carbolic acid and water, one part of carbolic acid to fifty parts of water.

Earth floors should be removed to depth of at least three inches or deeper if saturated with drainage and new earth or cement substituted.

Do not apply whitewash and consider disinfection complete. Germs are well preserved under a coat of whitewash and cause trouble after whitewash peels off. So destroy the germs with carbolic spray before applying the coat of lime.

Let the light into the stables; it is death to many disease germs.

Chapter XXVI.

ROUND-UP.

The higher the aim in dairying the better the achievement.— John Tucker.

Aim high!

Keep in mind the milk record of the noble Holstein-Friesian cow, "Pietertje 2d"—over 30,000 pounds in one year!

The Jersey cow, "Princess 2d," produced 46 pounds and 12½ ounces of butter in seven days! "Bisson's Belle," a Jersey, yielded 1028 pounds of butter in a year!

Do not be contented with the present United States average of only 3000 pounds of milk and less than 200 pounds of butter per year.

These high marks cannot be equaled, perhaps, by ordinary methods, but the low marks can be exceeded, to a certainty, by any dairyman who will study his business.

Holstein-Friesians and Jerseys are not the only cattle with great American records.

Dairy herds are improving, but I cannot help noticing many scrub cows in the fields. Bank robbers I call them.

Scales and the Babcock test are the enemies of the scrub cow.

The silo will become universal, of course; and peas will be used for silage as well as corn.

The thoroughbred bull will push the scrub bull to the wall, and the home-raised cow will increase in favor.

Advance in the science of breeding and feeding will be accompanied by advance in factory work. The factory system is not yet on a settled basis. Much is yet to be learned about separators, about butter making, about cheese making, and about marketing.

The wisely-fed calf will make a gain of a pound in live weight for every pound of digestible dry matter in the food ; and animals two years old will gain a pound of flesh for every ten or eleven pounds of digestible dry matter fed to them.

To sum up the whole matter, I look for future dairy profits to come from better cows, from careful weighing and testing of milk, from scientific and hence economic feeding, from superior and well-marketed products, and from good care of the manure.

Below are given the secretaries of the various Cattle Clubs and Breeders' Associations of the United States from whom information may be obtained:

Aberdeen-Angus, Thos. McFarlane, Harvey, Ill.
American Holderness, Truman A. Cole, Solsville, N. Y.
Ayrshire, C. M Winslow, Brandon, Vt
Brown Swiss, S. Fish, Groton, Conn.
Devon, L. P. Sisson, Wheeling, W. Va.
Dutch Belted, H. B. Richards, Easton, Pa.
Galloway, F. B. Hearne, Independence, Mo.
Guernsey, Wm. H. Caldwell, Peterboro, N. H.
Hereford, C. R. Thomas, Independence, Mo.
Holstein-Friesian, F. L. Houghton, Brattleboro, Vt.
Holstein-Friesian (Western), J. H. Coolidge, Jr., Galesburg, Ill.
Jersey, J. J. Hemingway, 8 W. 17th St., New York, N. Y
Polled Durham, J. H Miller, Mexico, Ind
Red Polled, J. C. Murray, Maquoketa, Iowa.
Shorthorn, J. H. Pickrell, Springfield, Ill.

DONT'S.

Don't have the stalls so low at either end that the internal organs gravitate from their proper positions.

Don't have feed or water troughs so deep that animals cannot reach the bottom without discomfort.

Don't forget to have the new cement floor of stable roughened to prevent slipping.

Don't allow cold wind to blow on cattle through cracks and openings in stable wall.

Don't forget that continued good health requires proper feeding, good air, sunlight and exercise.

Don't adopt for a feeding motto "Something for nothing." Feed much and doctor little.

Don't allow the cows to be pestered by flies. Pasture at night only, if the flies are unbearable.

Don't turn the cattle in the wet or frosted clover; it may cause bloating.

Don't strike or chase a cow with an apple in her mouth, she will swallow quickly and may choke.

Don't allow cows to eat decayed or old, withered potatoes; they contain a poison which is very fatal.

Don't throw bones where cows can get them; they will likely become fast in the throat or mouth.

Don't allow paint cans or painters' rags within reach of cattle; lead poisoning is generally fatal.

Don't allow cattle access to large quantities of salt; they will sometimes eat enough to result fatally.

Don't allow cattle in the orchard. They destroy the trees, and the fruit if large may choke the animals.

Don't invite foul claw by allowing animals to stand in stagnant water, mud or filth.

Don't compel animals to drink dirty, stagnant or icy water.

DON'T RUN THE COWS.

INDEX.

Aberdeen-Angus Breed	17	Hides	96
Abortion	138	Holstein-Friesian Breed	15
Ailments and Remedies	131	Hoof Distemper	136
Analyses of Feeds	51	Hoven	134
Ayrshire Breed	14	Inflammation of Udder	132
Babcock Milk Test	109	Jersey Breed	13
Beef Clubs	92	Kickers	133
Beef, Cuts of	108	Lice and Ticks	136
Bloat	134	Lockjaw	37
Breathing Organs	135	Lumpjaw	139
Bronchitis	135	Manure, Care of	55, 97
Brown Swiss Breed	18	Milk Fever	138
Butter Colors	77	Milk in Jars	104
Butter Increasers	82	Milk Preservatives	69
Butterine	81	Norfolk Polled	18
Butter Making for Novice	78	Oleomargarine	81
Buttermilk	96	Oxen, Training	37
Calf, Feed for	32	Pleurisy	136
Cattle Clubs	142	Pneumonia	136
Cheese	83	Ration for Dairy Cows	44
Choking	134	Red Polled	18
Colic	135	Rheumatism	139
Constipation	135	Ringworm	136
Creamery, Floor Plan of	120	Scours	135
Dairy Appliances	109	Shorthorn Breed	16
Dehorning	28, 128, 133	Silage, Analyses of	101
Devon Breed	16	Sore Teats	136
Digestive Organs	134	Sore Throat	135
Disinfection	140	Sprains	137
Durham Cattle	16	Sterility	138
Dutch Belted Breed	17	Sterilized Milk	70
Ensilage	48	Suffolk Polled	18
External Cow, Parts of the	9	Texas Fever	140
Founders	135	Tuberculosis	139
Galloway Breed	17	Veal, Cuts of	108
Garget	135	Vices	132
Generative Organs	137	Warts	136
Guenon Theory	27	Wolff's Feeding Table	43
Guernsey Breed	14	Womb, Inflammation of	138
Hereford Breed	15	Wounds	137

www.ingramcontent.com/pod-product-compliance
Lightning Source LLC
Chambersburg PA
CBHW030307170426
43202CB00009B/901